MW00936670

Situations
OF THE
Heart

Situations
OF THE
Heart

EIGHT REAL-LIFE STORIES
OF INSPIRATION AND LOVE

CATHY JONES

XULON PRESS

Xulon Press
2301 Lucien Way #415
Maitland, FL 32751
407.339.4217
www.xulonpress.com

© 2021 by Cathy Jones

All rights reserved solely by the author. The author guarantees all contents are original and do not infringe upon the legal rights of any other person or work. No part of this book may be reproduced in any form without the permission of the author.

Due to the changing nature of the Internet, if there are any web addresses, links, or URLs included in this manuscript, these may have been altered and may no longer be accessible. The views and opinions shared in this book belong solely to the author and do not necessarily reflect those of the publisher. The publisher therefore disclaims responsibility for the views or opinions expressed within the work.

Unless otherwise indicated, Scripture quotations taken from the King James Version (KJV) – *public domain.*

Paperback ISBN-13: 978-1-66282-111-0
Ebook ISBN-13: 978-1-66282-112-7

Dedicated to my children
TreVaughn, Ryan,
Felicia
Lawrence Jr and Marques

TABLE OF CONTENTS

PREFACE

Through the challenges and hardships, I have found that it extremely easy to fall into the negative and that can make things rather tough. I needed to reach inside and find some of the good things that brought me to where I am today. It's those small times we often forget about that make us laugh hysterically or family members that make everlasting impressions on us. Jami the Nurse is a wonderful example of how drug-addicted babies can become successful with the proper nurturing and how Brendon managed to get the squirrel out of the house. The Hotdog Excursion shares the fun times' sisters have grown up in the childhood home The Outing is a great adventure of travel and seeing life in many ways. A Feeling Forever is a love story that will leave you wanting more of that feeling. These are just to name a few. It was put on my heart to write these stories because I had been going through some hard times and then one day it came to me that there were not enough positive, fun, encouragement, and inspirations in my world, or around me and that is not all that has made me the writer I love to be. I hope that you laugh too, be inspired, and feel the love throughout these stories.

Please continue reading on to enjoy the rest of the stories.

And may God bless you all.

HER DREAM

Genesis 37:9

And he dreamed yet another dream ad told it his brethren,
And said, Behold, I have dreamed a dream more;
And, behold, the sun and the moon and
The eleven stars made obeisance to me
King James Version Old and New Testaments

*L*ynn is a virtuous, tall, smart red-headed woman who lived in a small town. She had made a vow one day that she would grow up and get her life on the right track. She was going to pursue the passion she had for writing that God had given her, but addiction got to her first. Writing has been a desire she has had all her life. She knew all her life that one day she was to become a successful author. She started writing at an incredibly young age and she was always writing down some of the dumbest things that eventually ended up being part of her good work. She was a year old with her first piece of paper in her hand. Every day after that she carried her journal and matching pens with her all the time. It became her dream.

Lynn's mother Silvia would always set aside the perfect paper for her because she was so little. She got a hold of a black piece of construction paper one time and ended up with the black ink all over the place, her face, and on her clothes Whenever Lynn was up playing around, she always wanted her mother's paper. Silvia never could figure out what it was that made paper so appealing to her but, she always had a special one just for her. There were so many times when she did not want to write anymore, but she continued even though she was frustrated by the obstacles in front of her. However, there was always something that would tug on her heart to keep her going. She was going to throw it away and then decided she would just leave it all in a duffle bag where it started to get some mold on them. Even still, her work ended up being an exceptionally large collection. Over two-thousand pieces of work had accumulated. However, she inherited the disease of addiction. It unfairly held her captive for most of her life and her desire to write had to be placed on hold. It has been on hold for quite some time now but the thought of her following through with her goals stayed with her no matter what she was going through or where she was. It is still with her today.

Lynn loved writing so much that she kept making promises and more promises to her family about her doing something good with her talent for writing. She knew she was going to make it into the writing world or maybe even write music one day. This sounded a little crazy to everyone around her because she was not in any way in the right place for those goals to be reached. Nevertheless, it meant so much to her that she kept trying repeatedly to put something together with writing, but it never was finished. It appeared to everyone that she wanted to do the right thing in her life but when life got in the way, the addiction stood at attention ruining any of her chances to turn the tables. She was going in and out of many treatment centers but none of them was what she needed to be successful.

She never lost hope for herself or lost any tenacity that one day she will be living a healthy lifestyle and doing what everyone has always said she never would, to write professionally.

Then one day, on her last attempt to get the help she needed, she collapsed to her knees, not just asking God to get her out of that situation but heal her body and to put her disease to rest. Lynn surrendered her entire being to God that day and things began to change. Everything she did was different than she had ever done before. That was when she found the spiritual guidance inside that she needed that successfully put her disease to rest. Nevertheless, Lynn did not go back to her writing right away. There were too many fear factors of loss in the past that she was not ready to bring back up again just yet. She went on to build a new life with her children and husband. She also went back to school and got her education.

Ten years later, Lynn was finally stable in her life and felt as if she was complete when she started feeling the desire to write again. This made her nervous because she had to decide whether it was time to face her fears of bad choices, abuse, and extreme loss of loved ones, or not. It was a lot to process all at once. There were going to be tough areas to walk through for her to get back to what she loved to do the most, writing. Her goal was to be a successful, published credited, author and/ or possibly write music one day. She went to pick up that pen for the first time then paused, sitting quietly and nervous. As she began twiddling the pen in her right hand, she was feeling the paper with the other hand. Scared inside, anxiety grew and grew. She was going through flashes from the past, all of them traumatic situations, but soon Lynn realized she had come too far to let old demons get in her way.

She put positivity in her head immediately reminding herself just how strong and beautiful of a person she was today, and that God planned this just for her. Saying that repeatedly to herself, she now had to decide to put her work away forever or decide if it was going to be worth fighting for in the end this time. There was no going back.

Lynn's passion for writing had been inside her always and she was not going to stop doing something she loved so much. That was the one thing that allowed Lynn to be herself. Therefore, she took a big, deep breath, looked at her husband, smiled, and started writing the first piece in over 13 years. It felt so good to have broken through such a barrier! It was as if a weight was lifted from her and joy was returning! There was nothing that could stop her now! She began working on pieces again and put the work she had already saved into small manuscript collections. She fearlessly began submitting her work to contests or with companies that were looking for the poetry and short story work now that she was working on those too. Even though nothing has yet to be recognized for any real writing, she refuses to quit and loves what she does. It had become a big struggle for Lynn, as to how she was going to get her work out to the public without it being taken or used without her permission.

She worked a lot on the computer. There are a lot of writing companies that are not so honest out on the internet, so research was particularly important. This was also a fear that Lynn had to overcome, probably the hardest one yet.

This was troubling her so much that she began having trouble sleeping at night. Her mind just could not shut off about the whole situation! She became more tired by the day with increasing mental exhaustion by the hour. Being sleep-deprived, she would toss and turn at night when she did try to lie down until she could no longer fall asleep at all.

The next day she went back to work trying to find a way to get to her breakthrough. With no luck and her pattern of sleepless nights recently, Lynn thought that if she took a light sleeping aid it could help her get the rest she needed to refresh her thought process and be sharp as a needle for the next day's work. Not shortly after taking the aid, she had finally begun to drift off to sleep. Lynn began to dream.

It was dark and foggy. "I thought I heard something outside my window." Lynn heard herself saying. Across the room behind the sheer curtains, I saw a shadow of what appeared to be the outline of a woman. I could tell this because it was a smaller more petit figure than I thought a man would be. Instantly, I felt a familiar connection to this image. As if I knew it personally and loved it, but I could not place where I knew it. However, I know I have felt this kind of love before.

This abundance of fear-of-the-unknown had me trembling inside! It was convincing me that my dream goal and personal passion for writing would be taken advantage of and that it would pay another person greatly while I was left to struggle on my own. The feelings of deceit suddenly overwhelmed me! The hurt and pain grew and grew as I was left with only curiosity and my creative passion inside. The only thing that felt safe from whoever this was.

Just then another shadow drifted in next to the first one, this time, the image was much larger and somewhat stouter like that of a man. It appeared this image was together with the other one. It positioned itself slightly behind the smaller image and just stayed there as if it was protecting the smaller image. I soon realized it was a part of whatever this was too. I stood silently still, for what seemed like an eternity as if I were frozen in time when the feminine shadow slowly approached me. I was nervous and scared at the same time I just remained still trying to breathe normally.

It leaned in towards me to whisper into my ear, "Do this and you will receive your share of the treasures back". It was never made clear what I was supposed to do or what exactly the treasures were that I would get back. It went on to say in a deep authoritative voice, "You have not been ready until now. We have been paying attention to you for some time to see if you were ready and at first, we thought you were not going to make it. You were reckless and disrespectful. Those are not the qualities required. However, through your trials and tribulations, you have shown us just how much you have grown and that you are responsible enough to handle this now." I was so confused about my emotions, yet I felt very vulnerable to an unknown thief as if a knife had been stabbed into my back. It was as if I was physically being ripped into pieces one part at a time.

"Someone must have taken over on my identity and my writing work as well." I thought to myself. Who would do that? How did it get out into the world? There were too many things I wanted to know. But right now, I must do what they want so I can get what is mine. Everything I had worked for over all these years was rightfully mine and the whole time it is being dangled right in front of my face like a horse to a carrot. Unable to express the feelings I was experiencing at that precise moment, I reached out with one hand towards one of the dim-lit images; I felt like this was the one who would help get all my life's work back for me.

My heart was pounding so loud! I was unable to hear anything else around me. It was too hard to swallow with the knot in my throat that had been building for some time now. My chest felt heavy as the pain grew stronger until the feelings overflowed, allowing a single tear to run down my cheek. From what little breath I could muster up through the knot in my throat, I whispered, "Who are you?"

Instantly after asking that question I was instantly in another room, finding myself sitting in what appeared to be an office. It was dim under the soft lighting as I sat at an office desk. On top of the desk, there were flowers in the corner and a computer in front of me. It was as if I was in my own cubical with only three walls. I looked around trying to figure out where I was or how I even got to this room. There was a sign hanging from a tack on the wall that said, "The smallest voice can make it major" I just stared at that saying for a moment and then began typing whatever came to mind.

I do not know why I just started typing but I did as if it was what I was supposed to be doing. With every completed project came a reward just appearing out of the blue; office supplies, and whatever else was needed to assist me in completing the work. I was steadily trying to figure out what it was I was supposed to be doing to reach my break-through here. What was the "this" that the image spoke of and how was I going to find it? If I could not find it, how was I going to do it? So, I just kept writing and writing, completing piece after piece, and project after project. The ideas seem to stay coming one after another. I never left that room for what seemed like the longest time. Well, I think it was a room, but the only light was directly above me and darkness was everywhere around me off in the distance. I kept noticing the sign on the wall saying, "The smallest voice can make it major" This gave me hope and the desire to keep going!

I typed so much and worked so hard that I felt like my fingers were going to fall off! I felt I was just spinning my wheels because I had not reached where I wanted to be with my writing yet, successful! I still was not acknowledged as a credible writer and I had not encountered the dark images for some time now. I continued, writing, and preparing projects. I completed so many that it became somewhat overwhelming with them stacked all around me. I decided to try and step away from the desk for a moment but then realized that it was only the darkness that surrounded me.

I sat back down to the computer to continue to the next idea. The more I wrote and completed a piece of work this time, the darkness began to start showing some light. It became brighter and brighter around me until I was able to see off into the near distance. It was finally enough light for me to walk out into another section away from the small cubical I was in. The larger one of the two images appeared to be waiting for me off in the distance. "Have you done what has been requested of you Lynn?" I heard in a low strong voice. "What was it exactly that was requested of me?" I said in a lost voice. "I have been working my fingers to the bone for I don't even know how long, completing project after project, piece after piece, and for what, someone to take it?" The shadowed image stood silent for what seemed like forever. It created a strong, intensive vibe that was beginning to be very intimidating. When it came in closer to me; my heart started pounding again not quite sure of what it was going to do.

It then whispered, "We told you that you appeared responsible and that you could handle it all now, right?" it asked, "Well yes." I replied unsure of what was about to happen. "We also informed you that if you do this you would receive your share of the treasures, is that right?" it asked again, "Yes," I said in a humbling tone. "We gave what you needed to do what was requested of you to do. The office supplies to complete your work, the computer to work on, an isolated place for you to focus on your subject, and whatever else you could use to do the job, and you did. You did not create those projects for anyone to take

Lynn; you were doing the work for the job you have been wanting all along." I was shocked! "But why would you say that I would get my share of the treasure back?" I asked very curiously. The image replied, "Because when your work truly was able to get out into the world, it did become a success, but you were not ready, nor in a good place in your life at that time where you would be able to handle the responsibilities of being a good writer. We had to make sure that you were ready Lynn." "That sign that is hanging in the office?" "The smallest voice can make it major?" "Yes," I replied, eager to get the answers I had been looking for, for an awfully long time! It continued, "Your writing spoke very loudly and made such an impact on us and others that it did become major."

My heart sank right then and there! I could not breathe or move! All I could think of was, "Did I do it? I finally made it?" I thought I was going to explode inside with joy as I started trembling while tears filled my eyes. It became noticeably clear that what I had been looking for, I was looking at through negative eyes. This was the breakthrough I had been struggling for the entire time. I took a deep sigh to speak, "Oh thank you, but before you go, I must know, you said, "If you do "this", what was the "this" that you were referring to?" The image said in a proud tone, "Work, my talented one, work. You must do the work and show you can do the job! You did that, and you did excellently!" "Here is your share of the treasures and all that you have earned thus far." I was never happier in all my life! Tears of joy ran down my face like a faucet, gratitude was flooding me now. I was so thankful that there was someone who was looking out for me and not taking it from me the whole time. As I went to put my hand out to retrieve my treasures, the shadowy images began to fade and so did the treasure that was in its hands. "Wait a minute! You cannot go now! NO! NO! NO!"

I screamed. I was scrambling with both hands trying to reach the image with all my might. Shouting every second, I struggled with every effort to reach it, but it always seemed to be just slightly out of reach. Just when I thought I was going to grab it, it faded more out of sight. "I did not go through all of this to come up with nothing!" I said, screaming as loud as I could, fighting the whole way. "Wait a minute this was not the deal! I did what you requested of me and...

Lynn sat straight up in the bed, screaming NO! NO! NO! She was dazed and confused as to where she was for a moment until she looked around the room and realized, "It was me! The image was me the whole time." She calmly said in a low voice. Coming out of the sleep daze and realizing that she was at home, in what she knew was her bed and a few belongings such as her laptop on the table that she recognized as her own. Except now, everything around her including the bed was much nicer and fancier than she remembered it to be. Everything was new and cleaned with a holiday spice scent throughout the room.

Her bed was an eccentric four-post Arabian bedstead with egg white sheer curtains that hung elegantly from the railing. The room was mostly white, with earth tone colors browns and gold's that accented everything nicely in the Victorian theme. She paused for a moment taking the time to observe everything, and then slowly got out of the bed.

She was shocked and amazed as she walked slowly and cautiously with intentions of making it over to the main table that was over by the large bay windows across the room, admiring everything around her along the way. She noticed the gold-based lamp that sat on the marble top nightstand which was next to her bed. Then slowly ran her hand across the marble top dresser that matched her nightstand which held her antique mirror at just the right angle for her.

Lynn was in complete awe because this was none of the furnishings she had in her house before going to bed. Remembering her dream, she was trying to understand what it was trying to say to her. As she started looking up slightly, she saw that the huge painting on the wall was a hand-painted self-portrait of her created by an anonymous artist. As she continued around the room, she admired the burgundy lace, tie back curtains that hung over every window. The white angora rug was placed properly in the center of the room. When she approached the main cherry wood table, she walked along the outside of it touching the many surfaces, noticing that it was exceedingly long and was able to seat eight. She spotted a few things spread out over one whole end of the table that was closest to her. The furthest part of the table was neatly set with fine china, wine glasses, and silverware that were wrapped in gold napkins with burgundy rings.

Lynn went around the table slightly brushing her fingers on the edge of the china, and then picking up one of the crystal wines glasses to admire it then gently placed it back on the table. She could not believe that this was all hers! Or was it? Where did it come from? She wondered as she continued around the other end of the table where she noticed a laptop. It was open to a word document. There was a notebook next to the laptop with chicken scratch notes all over it, pens of many colors, and a lot of sticky notes stuck to everything. Lynn could not believe what she is seeing with her own eyes. Was this all hers? Was she really in her house or was she still asleep? Well, she must be awake because she was able to touch things around the room and feel them, she thought. Glancing off to the other side of the table she noticed a newspaper and a couple of books. Curiously, she found herself walking her way around to the other side where she sat bewildered at the head of the table. She reached out to pick up one of the books and when she saw what was written on the page she fell back into the chair in utter shock! The book sat resting on her lap and in it read, "Blessings in Disguise" written by Lynn White.

JAMI THE NURSE

Luke 1:42

And she spoke out with a loud voice and said,
Blessed art thou among women and
Blessed is the fruit of thy womb
King James Version Old and New Testament

*J*ami is a young, vibrant woman who has always wanted to make a difference in the world. She loved to help others.

The daily check-in at the local hospital was being done on the maternity ward when Jami the nurse noticed that there was a red flag alert on a patient named Lacey D. She was a known addict on her third kid who was still trapped in her disease. It was close to her delivery date and it had been a while since anyone responded to the alert, so the nurse asked around to see if that woman had come in or had the baby yet.

Lacey was flagged for leaving a treatment center while she was pregnant. Anywhere she went to have that child the authorities or family or whoever is primary contact had to be notified and she and the baby must be held at the hospital until further notice. This was a statewide alert so there was nowhere that she would be able to go without being detected. No one in the maternity ward knew anything about the red flag or if she had the baby or not so she just took a mental note of the whole situation and continued to her rounds. The nurse was almost to the room where she was working when it got super loud. Suddenly the emergency door swung open; "we need a room now this baby is coming!" they sat the woman down in a wheelchair as she was screaming, "The baby is coming!" as they rushed her off to a room. They got her prepped to deliver and notified the doctor. When the doctor entered the room, he announced to the others, this is a red flag. Everyone was on the same page. It made sense now why that alert showed up.

It was early in the morning when Lacey's contractions became closer and closer. The nurse on duty was doing everything she could to make things as comfortable as possible for her. "Ayah, whoa, whoa, whoa, ayah" she breathed in between contractions. "OK sweetheart." The nurse said. It looks like we have a little one who is insisting on coming two and a half months early! Just keep breathing. "Ayah, whoa, whoa, whoa, ayah" she kept breathing. The baby's head was already beginning to show. Lacey was five feet nine inches maybe 140 pounds and that was pregnant. You could see her ribs and the baby appeared ridiculously small. Lacey was malnutrition and dehydrated which made her stomach look like it was vacuumed packed around the baby.

It was sad because you could see every little detail of the baby's body and limbs. She was nothing but skin, bones, and the baby was not moving. It was in distress, but they did get a heartbeat, a faint one but they got one. "Ayah, whoa, whoa, whoa, ayah" she kept breathing while screaming in pain. There was truly little water that broke so that concerned the nurse. This baby was coming and coming fast! The nurse had just enough time to halfway wash up before, "AAH!" "This baby is coming!" Lacey yelled. She grabbed her legs to hold on as she had no choice but to push. The nurse turned her head to see what was happening and instantly she rushed to the table because she saw the head crowning. Just as she reached out, the baby came shooting out like a rocket. The nurse caught her in one hand and arm. She called for help and it was not long before the hospital room was filled with doctors, nurses, and now family.

One of the nurses on the team pointed out to the doctor that the new baby girl was blue around her nose and mouth due to a lack of oxygen. He acknowledged with a nod to the nurse in awareness then rushed the baby out of the room. Lacey was an addict so they had to hurry to get the baby into the ICU incubator before any complications could arise. The baby girl was born addicted to crack cocaine two and a half months early and they were afraid of complications due to the severity of Lacey's addiction. The baby weighed only 5lbs, but after they got her in the incubator, she started to lose weight dropping down to 4lbs 5oz. It was scary for a minute because the baby would not eat, and she was steadily dropping weight.

The nurses stayed watching her twenty-four hours a day. The father Larry joined Lacey. They could visit and sit in the nursery with the little one but they were not allowed to have her in the room or outside, or anywhere it was not supervised. Everyday Lacey and Larry would take turns sitting together holding this baby girl close to them for hours at a time. Larry would show up first thing in the morning, go check on their baby girl, and then make his way to Lacey's room. Lacey was the love of Larry's life. Seeing his love go through this crushed him. He took every opportunity to try to make things better for them both; however, Lacey was sick with a disease that could never be fixed. She will have to deal with that her entire life no matter how much Larry needed to fix her. The time that they did have together was quality time for them while they took every chance, they could have with their baby girl.

Lacey was back in her room for the routine vitals after having a baby. While she was talking to the doctor, she brought up breast-feeding, thinking that would get her more time together with her baby girl. The doctor left to go make sure that this was going to be ok but when he came back into the room he explained; "unfortunately by law, I am not allowed to let you breastfeed the baby." Lacey began crying, "Why can't I feed my baby!" she just kept yelling at him. He calmly said, "The level of crack cocaine in your system is extremely high. It has gone through your whole body. Meaning that it has contaminated the milk you have and will contaminate the milk you produce until all drugs are out of your system. The levels are so high that if you fed her you could be charged with contributing to the delinquency of a minor." She looked at him stunned, "what?" she said in disbelief "how can that be?" The doctor came in a little closer and said, "You are producing liquid cocaine for milk and would be feeding her drugs all over again." She laid there and cried so hard knowing she was going to have no other choice but to sign her rights away to her daughter.

The little one had some challenges she was going to be facing, but for now, the doctors came in to talk to Lacey's sister Susan because she was going to be the one taking her home. "Little one will be going through some pretty hard withdraws." The doctor started out saying, "We would like to give her something to help with that." The doctor said. Susan perked up, "No, I do not want another drug to reach this child's system! Then I must wing her off those too, no thanks. She will get through cold turkey." After the doctor explained all the bad things that could happen to little one, they came to an agreement that she would need oxygen-breathing treatments and some digestive aid because she was going to have a lot of tummy aches. Susan was told to expect a lot of crying. It took the little one longer than most babies in some areas like rolling over and sitting up due to her breathing and lack of oxygen. Susan got her out of the woods with her breathing, but she struggled with digestive issues, tummy aches, and constipation. The constipation was so bad she tried to clamp her cheeks together just to hold it in. It was severe for a little one. Susan practically had to regulate her bowel movements with suppositories and fruits and veggies as the little one got older.

Susan walked the floor many nights because little one would not stop crying even though everything was ok with her. She was not hungry, fed her. She was not wet and did not need to be changed. She was irritable from withdraws and it was extremely uncomfortable for her. Susan slept when little one slept, and spent half of her time at the doctor with her. She even quit her day job to care for the kids because of the little one.

Little one grew fast and beautiful. She flourished in middle school being a cheerleader, breaking heart after heart. She worked hard to graduate from high school at the age of 15. She had her first long time relationship that ended in yet another heartbreak, for him. By now Lacey had cleaned up and was able to visit more often. But only if she were doing well, if she wasn't doing well, she could not talk to the little one. The little one always liked things that helped people or fix people. She loved to play doctor with a stethoscope and Popsicle sticks for tongue compressors. All her dolls were doctors and all her dress up stuff was medical related. Every time someone skinned their knee, she was there with a band-aid and wet toilet paper. Her family and friends did not always want to be her patient so she would tell them,

"Ok, when you get sick don't cry to me." It was so funny because she sounded just like Susan.

As the little one blossomed into a wonderfully beautiful young woman, she experienced internal issues there as well. She went through some hard times with cysts on her ovaries and the possibility of not being able to have children. This frightened her and made her angry with her biological mother. If her mother had not been an addict, she would not have these problems. (So, she thought) The little one found her husband and was happily starting her family, but she was worried about her body, and if her mother ruined that for her or not. They wanted to have children but were having no luck. The cysts were getting worse, larger and one busted on her sending her to the hospital. Her doctor told her that her chances of getting pregnant were slim. However, with regular checkups, he noticed that the cysts were descending.

Then one day she went to her doctor's appointment like normal and all the tests were in. "Well, that huge cyst is finally gone and most of the small ones have subsided. I am, however, proud to tell you, Congratulations! You and your husband are pregnant!" The little one could not speak, she could not move, and then she said, "Is the baby going to be ok with my ovaries like they are? How far along am I? Are you sure? The doctor laughed at so many questions at once. "Yes, the baby will be fine now." She looked scared and asked, "Now?" "Yes, if the cysts didn't do any damage to the ovaries and you get pregnant, they should slow way down if not goes away altogether." He reassured her to not panic.

The little one did not handle pregnancy very well, a real bearcat that one. However, she did very well have her first baby girl. Now she had her family growing and was happier than anyone had ever seen her. Once the baby was old enough for her to be able to leave her, she went back to school. She wanted to go into the medical field of course. Still undecided of what she wanted to do she started with the medical basics until he had an idea of what field she wanted. During this time, they got pregnant with their second baby, another beautiful baby girl.

She was managing a husband, a home, and now two beautiful baby girls of her own. The whole family was enormously proud of her because she did not follow the patterns of her addicted siblings. It was a different story when they would drink. Sometimes that got way out of control, fights, blood, it was not ok. Susan was always afraid of her getting the addictive gene, just like her sister had. There were so many fights about going down the same path as her biological mother, but it did no good.

By this time Lacey went to treatment and had gotten clean and turned her life around. She slowly started coming back into the family and her only baby girl's life. Lacey was able to be there for the births of her grandchildren and was visiting often. Lacey gave her little girl the lecture about drinking and addiction but, that became very loud. She finally released what she was feeling.

The little one was not one to put all her feelings out there. She kept a lot of them to herself or she shut down completely. She told her mother, "I am glad that you are doing well and are back in our lives but, I am not you and I do not do drugs!" That hurt her mother so, she just looked with tears starting in her eyes and leaned into her daughter, feeling a profoundly serious moment between them. She said, "I love you more than life itself, but I am sorry, you are too me!" She sat there almost stunned, thinking. Her mother continued, "Unfortunately you are your father's child too and whether you like it or not, baby girl, your chances of becoming an addict are extremely high. With that said if you do not want to end up as I did, you will make sure to be responsible with it. I love you sweetheart and I am so very sorry you had a bad start in life but even with all the odds against you, you have beaten the odds and have exceeded expectations on all levels. "I am not going to do that mom." She looked at her. "I love having you in my life and I don't ever want to lose you to that stuff again." "I cannot make any promises to you, but I can tell you that is not an option today. Even if it was an option, it is not my choice. I want to be here to help prevent you from ending up like me. "OK".

It was hard for little one to hold on there for a minute. Drinking all the time, fighting a lot, it was creating marital problems and things just started getting out of control. Lacey was visiting while her first grand-daughter was born. The little one had some friends come down for the weekend and wanted to go out for the night, so they asked Lacey to watch the kids. "Of course, I will. Just make sure you guys don't get in any trouble." "Oh no, we are not going to be doing a lot, just a few drinks and we'll be back." It was going on midnight when there was a huge bang on the front door. Lacey made sure the kids were ok and went over to the door. "Who is it" It was her friend's husband. "Let me in." She cracked the door slightly when he pushed through the door. He was all beat up and bloody. His clothes were torn, and his face was dirty as if he planted it in the dirt, face first. "Where are my kids?" he said drunk and staggering. "Oh no, you can't come in here and wake the kids. They are fine." He was not hearing anything right now. Lacey thought to herself, "Dam! They messed this guy up!" She had to ask. "What happened to you?" He got loud and Lacey tried to keep him as quiet as possible, but it was no good. "They beat my ass!" She tried hard not to laugh at this man. "Who did that?" She asked while she got him a cold washcloth for his face. "Those guys!" he said. "Little one and those guys did it?" "Yes!" Lacey could not believe what she was seeing or hearing at this point. He eventually went outside and sat directly in front of the door with his head in his hands. She quickly shut the door and tried to contact her daughter immediately. She kept calling back to back over a hundred times. Lacey had that man kids! She did not like the fact that these kids put her in A position like that.

It becomes serious when children are involved. She was getting madder by the second. Little one called back, and Lacey answered, "What hell baby girl? I got this man drunk, mad, and all bloody on your doorstep wanting his children. He says you guys are the ones that beat him up!" "I know mom, do not let him take the kids anywhere!" she said quickly. "Well, no doubt girl! This man is lying across your one step out front! He is no shape to take any kids!" "What the hell happened and when are you going to be here to get this man in check?" "Mom, he was warned about treating his wife wrong and he wouldn't stop. My husband told him he was going to kick his butt if he did not stop treating his wife so disrespectfully. Then he made the biggest mistake and slapped her! He got his butt beat, just that simple." Little one heard giggling in the background. "Are you laughing mother?" Lacey busted out she could not hold it any longer. "I gave the man a cold washcloth to wipe some of the blood off his face. You guys did some damage to that man girl." "Well, you don't treat your wife like that around these guys." She said. She had Lacey tell that man to meet them down the road somewhere and that they were not angry at him anymore. At first, he did not want to go anywhere with them, and he wanted his kids to go home. He was going to take them so the mother would not know where they were. Lacey could not have that, nor could she allow them kids to go anywhere with that person. It did not matter if they were his kids or not. They came first. So, after Lacey told him to go to them, she locked the door and just kept telling him that she cannot let him in without them guys there, so he had to go. He did. He left and then not too long after that Lacey's kids showed up.

"Oh, my goodness! What did you guys do to this poor man? They went into all kinds of things this man did in the club, at dinner, and now after hours. "He slapped his wife on the dance floor, he said she needed to eat on the floor like a dog and kept calling her names all night long until we just could not take it anymore. It all had to do with him abusing his wife and little one's husband and his friend was not about to stand by and let him get away with that. He tried to fight them, so they whooped his butt.

This was enough when she saw the hurt on those babies' faces and all the hurt her friend was going through. Would he have done that if they were not drinking? Was he like that all the time? The little one did not know, and her friend was not about to tell her all of it. The very next day they went home and little one sat back that night and realized that it was going out of control. This time Lacey was involved and situations like this were not something she put herself around anymore. That made little one feel bad. "Do you see how damaging out of control drinking can be?" Lacey asked her daughter. "Yes, I do now, and we will slow down. "Honey", Lacey started to say. "This is how I got started into a major disease that almost took my life and it could yours too. Please be careful. It will sneak up on you and by the time you realize you are in trouble it will be too late, and you may not be able to stop." "I will mom." Little one replied.

The little one was not going to have anyone tell her that her behavior is the same as Lacey's. Not for a minute! So, she made sure she backed off drinking a lot and focused more on her family and her career. It took her traveling back and forth between two states just to get the education she was looking for. She had multiple sitters for the girls and she and her husband barely got to see each other as he would work four on three off or whatever the work required. They took the time for each other every chance they got. Sometimes it would get so busy scheduling a date night was necessary.

The little one went on to graduate from college with her entire family behind her, even her biological mother was able to share that wonderful moment. As much as everyone tried their hardest to be there for her, she was going to make sure that she was able to help others and help fix what was broken.

One day as Lacey was walking down the street and bumped into an old friend, "Oh, I see you had the baby." "Yes, I did." "What did you name her?" Lacey smiled a huge smile, "I named her Jami."

It Was in the Music

Genesis 41:8

And it came to pass in the morning that his spirit was troubled;
And he sent the and called for all the magicians of Egypt,
And all wise men thereof: and the pharaoh told them his dream;
But none could interpret them unto pharaoh
King James Version Old and New Testament

Cooper Day loved to live life to the fullest. He is a wonderful inspiration for children with Bi-Polar disease. There was not anything that Cooper would not try or anyone he could not love. However, he suffered from intellectual challenges constantly which made his daily routine difficult. It was hard for Cooper to understand as other children did. He needed to learn hands-on with things in life so he could see if he could do it. He may have been a little slow or even a little clumsy and it made him very uncomfortable as if he did not belong because the other kids began to stare at him in wonder with curiosity as to why this boy was the way that he was. He tried every day to find a way for him to learn that did not draw so much attention to himself. He knew he was different from the other kids; he just did not know why.

The music class made him the happiest.

We never knew when Cooper's moods were going to turn from good to bad. No one ever knew and some kids were already on the "pick on Cooper" team. So, almost every day was bad. It kept things hard when one minute he would be ok and enjoying life and the next he would be upset, frustrated, and unable to stop crying. He grew up as an only child and loved to be in his room a lot. That was his safe place, his comfort zone. He did not have any friends that he spent any real time with, mostly just kids from school and even then, he appeared to be socially different too. Almost everything was awkward to him. This made Cooper sad and so he would act out a lot in frustration by causing distractions by throwing things across the classroom or getting super loud. He could instantly turn that awkwardness into a class clown sort of scene.

When Cooper was told he could not do something and he was already set on that one thing, he had to do that one thing one way or another. There was no planning for another day because there was no other day for his plans. One night, it got late and so his mom Brenda was not going to be able to take him to the store that he wanted to go to earlier that day, "Cooper, we are not going to be able to go to the store tonight because they are closed now." "No mom! If we go right now, we can just get what we need and be back in no time." He would explain. "I am so sorry sweetheart, but they are not open." She would say stronger and sterner. "Come on mom, we need to hurry so we can get it in time." He kept on. "We cannot go, Cooper! They are not open, and we will have to go tomorrow." She yelled at him as she looked directly into his eyes so that he knew what she was saying to him. He would then stomp off into his room and slam the door. It just would not go through for him to understand. It was one-way thinking for him and that is somewhat how he functions regularly. He has come so far, being able to accept no when something cannot happen as planned. That does not mean that he will not try to debate the whole situation so that he is right on some level.

Along with everything else, Cooper also suffered from a sensory problem due to Autism that had him in a limited wardrobe. Shorts and a pullover hoodie were his favorite. His clothing had to feel a certain way against his skin otherwise he could not wear it all. Only certain material could touch his skin. There were no jeans what-so-ever! Tank tops and basketball shorts have been his wardrobe until it snows then he will find a pair of cotton sweatpants with the cotton sweat jacket that matches. He would get upset so easily that he would need to take time outs more than the average child and redirect himself when stress was high. Cooper loved to build things with Lego's, and he loved guns. He loved building guns out of Legos or whatever he could find. The guns he built worked too. They even had compartments for the clips and mags and he was able to cock it back and hear it click when you pull the trigger. If any of those things were moved in his room after cleaning, he would meltdown. Nothing can be moved in his room or it upsets him. He would be scared to not have what he needed when he worked on his projects.

Brenda started seeing different things about Cooper that were not being addressed such as, the clothes thing and in the beginning, Cooper had to eat a meal with a different utensil for each food. That food could not touch each other and if it did, it then became inedible. The requests from him were tense and no matter how hard his mother tried he insisted on having things the same way. This tended to bring more attention during school and other kids were finding him different so they would pick on him not understanding why Cooper was the way that he was.

The kids at school would tease him every day. But no matter how many times he said something to get help it continued. The bullying he was going through was taking its toll on him. He started seeing himself differently too. He was calling himself fat and saying things that the bullies were teasing him about, being ugly, or not being smart, only he was accepting these things about himself whether they were right or wrong. There were many names and teasing when he began to believe what others were saying about him even though none of it was true. This hurt him very much, but after a while, Cooper started seeing what they were saying about him. He began to believe all the negative things mean people say. Standing there in the mirror, looking into his own eyes, Cooper wondered why people would be so mean to him; after all, he didn't bother anyone and said next to nothing during school unless he was called for an answer. "Cooper", he said, "you're nothing that they think you are, God made you just right." And off he went to avoid the bullies at school yet again another day.

As it was, Cooper did not have many friends. Most of his activities consisted of music, writing, and singing. This is what he loved the most, over time it became a therapy process for him. The torture of going through school the way he had been was creating more damage by the day. He was depressed and sad, he hated going to school, and now he had a complex of what others thought about him, He would go into school and directly grab a seat in the corner. He minded his own business and did not bother anyone. But the anxiety remained. Cooper thought if he just stayed to himself that maybe they would leave him be or move to another kid to pick on. Yeah, that did not happen. It only allowed the bullies to tease him while he was sitting in the corner with nowhere to run. He took another teasing like it was a part of his educational routine or something.

"Hey, nerd I'm going to get you." A kid called to him. Cooper ignored this even though he knew he feared what these guys were going to do to him. He insisted on throwing things at Cooper. The pencils, erasers, balled up paper, whatever they could find that would not get them into trouble. He did not respond to any of this behavior. When class was over, he waited for them to leave before he started to move. It was lunchtime, and this was his opportunity to find a good spot out in the fields, alone with his lunch. It was such a relief not being picked on for a few minutes.

One day, as Cooper sat in those fields, he pulled out some paper and a pen and started writing, just writing about anything. It did not matter if it made sense or not, he just wrote and while he wrote, he always had a tune in his head. He would sing out loud or hum new sounds he could bounce around to. This not only removed the bad thoughts about him but made him feel better about the problems that he faced every day. Writing put Cooper in a place where he did not feel troubled. Everyone liked him, and he was not getting picked on or tortured. It took him to where he could experience a world that was the total opposite of what he was living every day.

The more he wrote about the trouble or the pain the more he released some of that anxiety and was able to deal with what he was feeling. He was finding hope and determination within his music. Cooper looked to the paper one day and noticed that he was writing poetry, a rhyming word here or there. It felt good! When he got home every day from school, he would go directly to his room just, so he could relax, write, and listen to music. He listened to songs that were uplifting, fun, about

31

caring for people, and of course, love. Who does not love a good love song? These sorts of music were able to calm the wrath Cooper felt daily from mean people. The words in the songs became a personal comfort zone for him. They provided the positive self-talk, encouragement, support, and love for others Cooper needed to make it through to a better day.

The more he wrote his pain into poetry, the more he could reduce his stress and get out how he was feeling about being bullied at school. Slowly, he started to say some of the verses he wrote about the bullies in his pieces to the bullies! Out loud! At first, they looked at him like he was totally off his rocker then continued to pick on him. The more he kept using his words to stand up to theses bullies the more the tables started to turn. Cooper's lyrics were positive and uplifting so it was not bad what he was saying about them it was good for them.

The next day, there was no trouble. Cooper was watching all day waiting for the ball to fall with these guys, but it did not. It just did not happen that day for the first time in a long time! He kept to this theory as it worked. Then Cooper wanted to know how good it really could make it now, so, he started putting a tune to some of these words he was throwing at these guys. This threw the bullies off. They teased Cooper still but nothing like what he was going through. It was getting better at school.

The more Cooper tossed out some lyrics to stay from getting picked on, the more the guys liked what Cooper was doing with the music. They knew it was about them for all the times they had messed with Cooper; however, his words were positive and changed how these guys looked at him. If they teased him about his clothes, he shot back with gratitude for the cloak. When they shouted inappropriate names, he came at them with, names are just names, that is how I am winning the game! The physical torturing had stopped completely. Cooper had managed to unknowingly challenge these bullies into something like a rap off, or dance fight only with words and tunes instead.

Everyday Cooper stayed with the music. He turned into a particularly good writer and songwriter, using his words to fight off bad for good. His mother started seeing changes in him that she was incredibly pleased to be seeing. His attitude changed about everything around him. He was no longer depressed, and she began to see smiles instead of frowns. Playing his favorite music when he got home inspired him to create more lyrics, dance a lot more, and show him how to look at himself better. Now when he looked in the mirror, he smiled and thought to himself, it was very, clever for him to stand up to a bully that way. Cooper was making the changes that he could not get help for in the beginning and it was working!

One day, Cooper sat way back in the fields like he always did. A tune in his head and poetry on the paper, when he hears slightly behind him, "Hey Cooper, can I join you?" It was the main bully! Cooper did not know what to make of this, so he had his guard up just in case it was another teasing. "OK." He said very nervously. "Don't worry; I didn't come here to tease you." The bully said. "Then why did you come here?" Cooper said very curiously. "I have noticed what you have been doing lately to get me and the guys to stop picking on you." "What?" he asked? "You are turning our bad behavior into a positive song." "Is that what you are doing here?" he asked. Cooper looked at him knowing that he could kick his butt at any moment, but he was willing to take a chance anyway. "Kind of, it's the same thing as a rap battle, have you heard of those?" "No, I just wanted to let you know that I am on to you and I know what you're doing."

Cooper sat still wondering what was going to play out. "OK." He said. Then he sat quietly doing the same thing he always did sitting out in the fields, writing. It was awkward! This is one of his bullies sitting next to him telling him he knows what he has been doing. "Now what am I supposed to do?" Cooper thought to himself. If he knows then how will I keep him from teasing me and picking on me?

The fear grew once more for Cooper. Then the bully said, "I have heard the words you have put together for when you are coming at us, they are rather good. I'll tell you what, I'm calling the dogs off, no more teasing and picking on you." "Thank you," Cooper said relieved. "You come to this address after school tomorrow. We have music in our blood too; I thought maybe my people could look over your stuff." Cooper was in shock! "What?" he could hardly help the shock and was not sure if this were just another prank to make him look stupid to everyone. "You're just teasing me again. Why should I believe you?" The bully sat quietly for a moment and then said, "Because nobody has ever got me to stop bullying them, with music! It's something I relate to like you and I know some people." It is nothing big. My family has been music lovers forever! I thought you were very clever coming at us like that, so you earned my respect. Maybe they will like some of your stuff." Cooper did not know how to take this, but it was nice. "Thanks, man." He responded in a cool voice. He put the address in his pocket and went about what he was doing.

"Steven." The bully said. "Excuse me?" Cooper asked, not hearing what he just said to him. "Steven," he said again. "That's my name, Steven." "Ok thank you, Steven." "You already know who I am, so we can skip that introduction!" They looked at each other and started laughing about the whole situation.

While Cooper's cleverness managed to resolve a serious issue, it was his secret that made it more enjoyable. The secret was that he had been using his music as a coping mechanism for his Bi-Polar. It brought him out of depression and contained the manic times. He applied the good words to the bad ones to take away the bad feelings of his everyday life. This was something only he knew but while he was learning how to use his music to get him through some of the hardest times of his life. He did it to balance out a day and pull himself out of incredibly sad days that, without his music, could have possibly turned out quite tragic.

Being bullied is a very scary event to experience. To have to manage the ups and downs of Bi-Polar and be bullied every day can lead many to suicide without proper support. Cooper took what was inside of him and applied what worked for him to feel normal or better. It was in the music where Cooper found his peace. It helped him verbalize in situations he otherwise could not, he found solutions to things that hurt him and was able to be open to new things and new friends. Cooper went on to write for Steven's family. But his music will always be his healing in a way that only the mind of a Bi-Polar person can, clever!

THE OUTING

Mark 16:12

After that, he appeared in another form unto two of them,
As they walked and went into the country
King James Version Old and New Testament

McKenzie is a twenty-nine-year-old, hard-working woman who had been working on her social connections to implement an idea on how to get her photography work published. She was building connections for potential job opportunities in the future. She always wanted to write or at least use some of what she already had to make a "bridge the gap" income. She did not think that anything would become of anything by doing this. As God would have it, it did not work out how she thought it would at all!

One hot summer day, McKenzie was sitting by the pool sipping on a cold drink and enjoying the kids when the phone rang, "Hello." She said with cheer in her voice. "Hi, can I please speak to Ms. McKenzie?" she heard from the genuinely sounding nice man's voice on the other end of the line. "This is she," McKenzie said. "I am Jordan from Mass Productions. I saw online that you're a writer and are looking to do something with your work or find an agent." The phone was quiet for a few seconds as she was stunned and could not believe her ears. "Uh, yes," McKenzie said sounding nervous. Her voice was crackling. He asked her, "What is it that you are looking to do with your work? McKenzie thought she had died and gone to heaven just then. "I am looking for an agent to help me turn my work into another income." She said very honestly. "Well, I prefer to meet with artists and get to know them before making any decision." He said to her. "I agree." She responded.

McKenzie was still relaxing in the sun as she tried hard to not jump for joy. Jordan was ready to make the move, "How about we look into a date and time that works for both of us when we can get together and talk more about what your goals are, and you can get to know me better as well. "That sounds great," McKenzie said so happy she was trying not to sound too eager. They agreed to check schedules and find a date that works so they can work out a place to meet. As it worked out, Jordan was willing to make the effort to go see McKenzie. So, she took a moment to do some research on this person and found that he knew some people that she knew so she asked about him getting two thumbs up before even letting him come to town.

It was a few hours to drive; however, he said it was lovely and the ride was relaxing. Once Jordan arrived in town, he texted McKenzie and they agreed to meet at a local restaurant in town. McKenzie arrived first. She never did like to be late because she did not like the attention it brought to her and she needed to prepare herself for who she was about to meet.

His picture on the business site was that of, "Oh my!" Because she arrived early to the restaurant, she was able to choose the perfect spot so she could see who was coming and going. A couple of people came and went and then out of nowhere here came this man who fit the description of, "Oh my!" She took in a deep breath as he got closer to the front door. Could that be him? She wondered. The first thing she noticed was the large beautiful cross that rested so nicely upon his bulging chest. This man worked out and was gorgeous!

"Ms. McKenzie?" "Yes, she said as she turned around and was speechless. He was, "Oh my!" He walked towards her with the most amazing smile on his face. He then leaned in to give her a hug and McKenzie was happy to respond to this handsome gentleman by hugging him back. All she could think was how great this guy smelled! They sat down at the booth together; he was still smiling at McKenzie. "You look very nice." He said. "Thank you." She said almost embarrassed. She was not used to getting compliments so when she did it was hard for her to see that. "You look great too," McKenzie said. "I love your cross; it's nice to see others who believe." "Thank you." He said looking down at it on his chest. This man was stunning, and he made it extremely hard to keep focused on the task at hand. There was a connection that neither one of them could understand. There was not a moment that they were not smiling at each other and as they got to know one another it became easier for them to start cracking jokes just playing around.

Jordan showed McKenzie how he was affiliated with many writing companies that covered him with everything he was working with. It was impressive, I must say; however, it was not only the credentials that made me want to go forward with this person. It was more. McKenzie shared with him about all the places she has submitted work and all the material that she had that was ready for publication. She was hoping that he would take her on with all that she has to offer. They talked for some time about more than just writing and working.

A special something was happening here that only God himself knew about. Jordan kept a smile on her face as he ordered himself a drink. "Would you like anything"? He asked. "No thank you". She declined politely and stuck with water to keep from embarrassing herself around this gentleman.

As they continued to share about themselves, they learned that they had a lot more in common than they thought they would such as the music, writing, and the whole process. Jordan offered her something to eat and she politely declined that too, this kept a smile on Jordan's face as if he were relieved to see someone who was not taking advantage of what this man could offer. McKinsey was content just being in the same room with this person.

After Jordan finished his drink, he was going to get a hotel room, but it appeared everyone was full. There was a calm to this man that only God could explain. The spirituality coming off him was radiant and shining bright. McKinsey stopped for the moment and focused on what her gut was telling her and what God would want her to do. After a few moments of silence and calls to everyone in town with no luck, she told him, "Well, you can stay at my place." It was very odd as to how calm it felt opening her home to him. Jordan took the couch after meeting the two kids and the dog.

The night was enjoyable, sharing what work McKinsey was working on and talking a lot about writing, publishing, and even God. Come the next morning, Jordan left before anyone got up to get an early start on the road back to the other side of the state.

He left a text message for McKinsey that read, "Hey, you were sleeping so nicely I did not want to wake you up. Thank you for opening your home to me when there was nowhere to stay. I will call you later." McKinsey did not know what to think. Did that wonderful night happen? Different, new, fresh, work, and opportunities. It was a blessing to find that they were looking for the same things and that Jordan was a great mentor.

Jordan came across as a very inspirational person and it was obvious that he had the lord in him just by the way his aura glowed on him and the way he was so kind and attentive. This man was a gentleman and it had been a long time that McKinsey has had an encounter with a good person with manners.

That day McKinsey spent the whole day with her head in the clouds thinking about what she had to do to be ready when the writing calls. Later, that night Jordan called her as he said he would. They talked for about an hour about what kind of work he wanted, and what to do with all the material she had. He pushed the book-writing more than sharing any information about writing music. Once they set a foundation of the relationship, they agreed to check schedules so they can get together again.

McKinsey was so excited she could barely breathe; however, they did manage to set a date to meet at the half-way point from each other's homes two-weeks out. The halfway point was about three hours from where she lived but it did not matter. McKinsey went crazy for the next two weeks trying to make sure she had all the work to impress this man. When the time came for her to leave, she was ready for almost everything. They went Dutch once arriving at the hotel. They got their keys and retreated to their rooms. It was nothing she thought it was going to be. It did not look anything like the website and most amenities were not available because of being broke down like the pool. They did the best they could to hold out for the first night. It was dirty and ran down and not to either one of their standards. "Would you like to go get some dinner?" Jordan asked. "Sure," McKinsey replied. "It is better than hanging out here." "I agree," Jordan said as he looked at her like that place was beneath him. It was not up to McKinsey's standards either. They went out to a wonderful, Mexican restaurant where they enjoyed a nice dinner topped off with a couple of drinks. The conversation was stimulating as McKinsey was all ears when he began talking about the writing business and some of the things that he has done in the past. She was trying to learn as much as she could. Jordan was a breath of fresh air because she felt he was honest from the very beginning. The evening was amazingly beautiful as they got to know each other, sharing what they were looking for in the work, the associations he carried, and the many organizations that he was involved with was a little overwhelming at first. It sure does take a team to get this kind of work done.

"So?" What do you want to do as an artist? Jordan said. "I would love to write music one day, but I am open to all avenues when it comes to my writing. "Sounds like a plan." "I want to help you be the best-selling author that I believe you are." McKinsey was skeptical about everything. She already did not trust men, so he was going to have to come correct. There was something about this man that gave McKinsey a sense of peace, or maybe it was a gut feeling to go ahead and take a chance with this person. It is extremely hard for McKinsey to find comfort with having to trust a man with her writing and he is associated with the music business. Who would trust that? Well, she was going to have to start somewhere with someone, so she chose to put her faith in this man and believe in him to come through with their success. It was getting late when they went back to their rooms. "Can I take you somewhere tomorrow? He asked her. "Ok, where?" she replied. "There is a wonderful park just down the way I think will be very inspiring for you." "Ok," McKinsey said, "until then," she said as she went into her room for the night.

It was a bright and sunny Saturday morning when McKinsey woke the next day. She prepared to do a lot of walking; however, she only had two pairs of shoes and neither one of them were tennis shoes. Yep, flip flops were the best bet. They both rode in his car down to the park where McKinsey could not stop looking around because there was so much to see. Jordan was a gentleman like I said, so he opened the car door for her, took her hand, and helped her out of the car. "It is beautiful out here Jordan," McKinsey said. Jordan watched McKinsey with a smile on his face, it was obvious he was enjoying his company. "I thought we could walk up the trail that leads to the river," Jordan said. "That sounds great," McKinsey said happily.

They began to walk along the exceptionally long sidewalk which went around a pond. In the center of the pond was a beautiful fountain. The ducks in the water made the whole look. There was a platform type dock that had a bench out at the end of it so that you can sit by the water; however, it was covered with bird poop so that was not an option. McKinsey and Jordan stood at the end of the dock looking out onto the water. It was so amazing, and the sound of the water was like music to my ears. "So, what is your story Mr. Jordan, because I know there is more to you than meets the eye." Jordan chuckled a little as if he knew I was right. "I have done some acting and have worked with some famous people here and there." I guess he was expecting a reaction but got, "That must have been a wonderful experience." She said calmly. McKinsey did not see this person as anything other than the person he was. Not fame, money, nor celebrity status was a factor in the friendship.

They continued to walk on going past the play center for the kids and then out onto another trail that went along the local river. It was a wide-open trail that had some large rocks along the banks. It was getting hotter outside, so they took a few minutes to go sit on one of the large rocks along the water. McKinsey did not have pockets to put her keys, so she was carrying them in her hands. They found a place to sit and shared a few stories. The waves were beginning to crash up against the rocks when McKinsey accidentally dropped her keys into the water. "Oh no!" She went into an instant panic because there would be no way to get another key.

"What am I going to do Jordan?" "Ok, calm down," he said as he started his way over to her. "Look where you dropped them." He told her. "Ok, it was right here under me," McKinsey told him. He climbed over a couple of rocks and positioned himself to where he could lift one of the rocks where she dropped the keys. "When I lift this, you put your hand directly down and slightly to the back." He told her. McKinsey was so scared to put her hands in there not knowing what was in there. She had no choice but to take a deep breath and do what he said to do. She reached down into the dark dirty water as he wanted her too, cringing the whole time, and to her surprise, she was able to reach right down, going directly to them and felt the keys instantly. She grabbed them quickly and got out of there just as fast. Jordan put the rock back down and said, "There you go." 'Oh, my goodness, I cannot thank you enough, Jordan." She told him sincerely "Don't panic and assess the situation. He said calmly to her. I noticed that the waves were going into the banks not out away from them that is how you were able to reach down and feel them. The waves pushed them back and luckily did not take them down the river. McKinsey was in awe of the way that Jordan handled that situation. It was like he knew right where to go to get her keys. She felt that God was with her right then, so she made sure to thank him more than once. She called moments like that a "God shot" Once McKinsey had her keys Jordan offered to hold them for her in his pocket. She politely looked at him in embarrassment and handed him the keys. They both started laughing at the whole thing.

They decided that that was enough for the rocks so they climbed back up to the trail where McKinsey could not lose her keys again. The trail ahead of them went along the river and could not have been any more beautiful. Lined with trees on the backside of the river, and in the parking area.

As they continued to walk it felt so easy to share their stories. He was not expecting anything, and neither was she. Conversations were so good that they had walked over two miles in just a short time as the evening fell upon them. "I have enjoyed this time with you." He said nervously. "I have too," she replied with a twinkle in her eye. They reached the end of the trail where they stopped to look out over the river and listen to the crashing of the waves.

It was amazing to feel so good with company that could stimulate the mind and not just the body. He was so much more to McKinsey than just a beautiful man with an exciting past. He was a fresh start into a new life with herself. McKinsey had met a lot of people in her life but none like this one, it was not about sex or personal relationships and it was something she wanted a lot more of. I think some would call it respect. McKinsey could not believe the great time she was having with this person.

I want more people in my life like this. She thought to herself as they walked side by side back up the river. "What do you feel like eating for dinner?" he asked her. "I do not know after a wonderful day like today, thank you," McKinsey said as she looked him in the eyes and began to blush the second his eyes met hers. "What sounds good to you?" she asked in return.

"I thought maybe some Mexican." He started to say but McKinsey interrupted with, "Oh my goodness that is what I was just thinking about." Jordan smiled at her because it was so cute the way they were on the same page without communication. They smiled at each other and agreed, "Mexican it is!"

The rest of the walk back was so enjoyable and relaxing. Loving the outdoors, and it was such a beautiful place. It was inspiring just as he said it would be, however, it was huge so half-way back they had to make a restroom stop, while she was sitting outside McKinsey realized the blessing she had in her life while watching the little ones that were running around playing. When Jordan returned to her they headed back to the car. "you ok"? Jordan asked. "It's perfect Jordan". She said with a smile.

The conversation was nothing but compliments about the day they had with each other as they drove back to their rooms. "this was a beautiful day Jordan, thank you so much for taking the time to be such an inspiration". Jordan looked at her and said, "you are more than welcome love, I enjoy your company." He pulled up to the hotel where they went in to go prepare themselves for a nice dinner out. They both showered, dressed up nice and then met each other outside.

"You look beautiful Ms. McKinsey," Jordan said the moment he saw her. "You do too Mr. Jordan." She replied with a smile. "Shall we?" He suggested "Absolutely," she replied. He walked around and opened his car door for her, then closed it after she was comfortably seated inside. He smelled so good it was distracting. He came around and sat in the car then looked at McKinsey, "I am enjoying myself with you McKinsey." He said sincerely, "thank you, I am enjoying myself as well." She said. He smiled and started the car, then headed out to the restaurant.

Jordan took a route to the restaurant that was so beautiful and full of nature and new sights that McKinsey had never seen before. "You have such enthusiasm about everything we have done today". Jordan stated. "It feels great too". She replied. They simply enjoyed each other's company with not too much said this time, just the great feeling they shared of being together.

Once they were parked, Jordan got out of the car and opened the door for her again. McKinsey was not used to all this mannerism. It was wonderful. He closed the door and then took her hand. McKinsey's heart jumped for a second, she instantly blushed. He smiled and took the lead and she was happy to follow.

He held her hand through the large crowd outside to the door of the restaurant where he let her go inside before him. The restaurant was busy and somewhat crowded, but it did not matter because once inside he took her hand again and led her to the bar where the last two seats were available. He pulled a high-back stool out for her and then ordered them both a drink.

McKinsey noticed that Jordan was the sort of person who could be very protective over the people he cares about just by the way he was so vigilant with her. The entire establishment was packed from wall to wall but that did not stop Jordan from getting us a seat and having a great time. He ordered a margarita and McKinsey ordered a B52. The bartender lined up some chips and some salsa and dips and they sat there for a while drinking slowly and snacking on what was in front of them. By the time they were done snacking they were not hungry either. McKinsey forgot what it was like to enjoy a night out. This was perfect.

They were heading back in their own directions the next morning, so they enjoyed the night they had. It was the little things that made them laugh together. Some of the things people were doing around them were extremely funny and the more they drank the funnier it all became. Jordan and McKinsey had the most compatible conversations there could be between them, she was wondering if this person was real or playing some game. Well, it did not matter when she let herself enjoy the here and now. "Are you still in the mood for dinner?" Jordan asked her. "Not really with all this snacking." She replied. "Ok." He said smiling at her. "I have had a very nice time with you Ms. McKinsey, thank you for meeting me." Of course." She said with enthusiasm. "I've had a wonderful time too, thank you for making this a time to remember. It was the perfect outing and I would love to do it again sometime." "Me too." He said looking her in the eyes. She blushed once again as they finished up their drinks.

They then decided to head out to go back to their rooms. But before they did, Jordan said, "There is somewhere I want to take you, you up for it"? She looked at him with curiosity and then said, "sure". "great"! he said and then he took her down to the water where they talked for hours about what she wanted with her writing and where she should start if she wanted to move forward with it. McKinsey took in everything he had to say, it was very intellectually stimulating but she also took the time to take in all the beauty God had put around her at that moment.

Sitting at the water's edge as they stared out onto the water. The moon was in just the right place to leave a mesmerizing glow upon the water. Their conversations simply flowed into each other's creating a connection they were both liking very much. They talked until we hours of the morning before heading to the hotel where they needed to get ready to leave the next day. Jordan approached McKinsey and said, "I have had the best day with you today. Thank you". And then he gave her a friendly kiss on the cheek. "Thank you, Jordan, I have had an amazing time". Then there was a slight pause before Jordan turned and she turned to go into their separate rooms.

The next morning, they met in the parking lot at their cars to say goodbye. "There you go looking good again'! Jordan said when he saw her. "Thank you, you are looking genuinely nice too. This was wonderful Jordan. I look forward to doing this again sometime." She said. "Yes, we should do this again." He replied. Then he kissed her on the cheek again, only this time she kissed his cheek back, and then he walked quickly around and opened the door for her to get in her truck. "Thank you again." Jordan gave her a hug bye as he shut her door and walked around to his car. They waved goodbye locking eyes for one last time and then drove out their separate ways home.

THE HOTDOG EXCURSION

1 Timothy 5:2

The elder woman as mothers;
The younger as sisters, with all purity
King James Version Old and New Testaments

O nce upon a time, there were two sisters, Stacy, 11, and Lynn, 6. Now, these girls were only five years apart and were close growing up. There were a lot of children in the home, so Stacy and Lynn had to share a room with bunk beds. They were the last two kids in the bunch. Stacy liked to keep her side of the room immaculate because she was OCD and did not know it. Well, Lynn was not. Lynn was Bipolar and did not know it. There were many squabbles and many pranks throughout the house and because they shared a room it was easier for Stacy to get Lynn and vice versa.

The weekend was approaching fast so it was a race to see who could ask for friends to stay the night first. There was no way their mother was going to let them both have a friend over, so they had to fight for it. Their mother Silvia asked them, "Do you have your room clean?" "Yes." Said Stacy. "No," Lynn said sadly. "That's not fair mom, she always has her stuff too clean all the time".

Lynn tried in her defense. "Sorry Lynn, Stacy can have her friend tonight and you can have one next time. Lynn madly ran to her room, sat on her bed, and pouted because she did not win this weekend.

Lynn then turned to her music and went about her day. She liked to play around on her bottom bunk by putting her feet up on the boards that went to Stacy's bed, the top bunk. This annoyed Stacy because it lifted her whole bed and it scared her. Whenever Stacy moved, she acted like she was going to get Lynn so Lynn would stop like she was asked just so Stacy would not come down and get her on her bed. One-time Lynn put her feet up on the boards and she lifted too high. The whole box spring and mattress fell onto Lynn's bed, with Stacy falling with it! Stacy ended up bonking herself on the head but not enough to be concerned about. Lynn didn't want their mother knowing what she was doing because she knew she would get into a lot of trouble. "Ow Lynn! What the heck are you doing"? Stacy yelled at her sister as she was climbing off the broken bed. "Now look what you have done"! "uh oh". Lynn said from under the bed that fell on her. We better get this back in place before mom comes up here or we are dead meat". Both girls pushed it back up into its place, so Stacy's bed was ok again. "Now stop putting your feet on my bed Lynn or I'm telling mom!" Stacy yelled at her.

Lynn decided that she was going to straighten up her things because Stacy's friend would be coming over and she would never get to have anyone stay the night if she did not. Once she was done with that, she put her favorite paper and pens on her bed and went outside to play with her friends. Stacy gladly shut the door behind her. A couple of hours had passed, and it was almost time for dinner. Lynn thought she better get back before Stacy and her friend got back at her for the bed move. The second Lynn walked into the house her mother yelled to her, "Lynn, go tell Stacy that Tamara is here." "OK mom!" she replied then she went to the bottom of the stairs and yelled as loud as she could, "Stacy you have company!" Lynn said in a jealous voice. "I could have done that Lynn, go play." Her mother told her.

"Hi, Tamara," Lynn said nicely. "Stacy is upstairs if you want to go up there." Lynn stayed sitting on the couch in the living room and watched some TV for a while. Stacy never wanted her in the room when her friends were over. That never really mattered to Lynn because she was the spicy one of the two and loved to be bold in her room and with her sister. There were, however, times when all of them did get along. Tamara was Stacy's best friend in the whole world. They loved to do everything together, even pull pranks on Lynn.

Tamara was friends with Stacy from kindergarten and was around our house so much at times we all were like sisters. Sometimes we got along and sometimes we did not. Lynn watched out when Stacy started being nice to her when Tamara was over. She knew something was up and that Stacy was going to get her in some way. They invited Lynn to play games with them until dinner was ready. She did, however, she kept her guard up.

"Girls! Come and eat!" mom yelled at the bottom of the stairs. They all ran down the stairs just so mom could say, "Stop running down the stairs!" They all grabbed their spots at the table and settled in while mom got drinks placed next to their plates. "Tonight's dinner; hotdogs and macaroni and cheese, something simple tonight girls". Mom said. "Thank you" they all said at the same time. They all started eating when Stacy started in on Lynn, making smart remarks like, "Better watch out tonight Lynn, you never know. Then she would just leave it at that to make her wonder what the heck she was going to do and how. "No, I better not Stacy. Lynn said looking her in her face as if that was a challenge. Stacy and Tamara started laughing because they knew they were messing with her.

Dinner was late that night as it was hot to cook in the kitchen so when dinner was done their mother said, "Girls, go get cleaned up for the night."

Lynn always had ketchup around her mouth when she ate hotdogs, so she went to go to the bathroom, but Stacy said, "older kids first" and walked right past her to the sink. "Stacy! Mom, Stacy cut in front of me saying big kids before little kids"! Her mother could not help but giggle because Lynn's face looked like the jokers with a ketchup smile while she is yelling about Stacy and her friend. By the time they were done in the bathroom Lynn was done fussing with her mom and went into the bathroom and got cleaned up.

While Lynn was doing her own thing Stacy and Tamara had other plans of their own. They snuck into the kitchen and each grabbed a hotdog to take to the room. "Hey, why don't we put these up her nose and take pictures while she sleeps tonight," Stacy said. Both girls laughed at the thought and put the hotdogs aside, so Lynn had no idea what was going on. Now, every time Tamara and Stacy came across Lynn they would laugh or giggle at her. Lynn started to wonder why they were doing that. "What are you laughing at me for?" Lynn asked. "Nothing," Stacy said. Then her and Tamara went upstairs to play, leaving Lynn behind.

Lynn was still frustrated at Stacy for being a brat while she was with her friend, so she stayed downstairs and watched some TV with her dad. "Stacy being mean again?" her father asked. Lynn just looked her dad in his eyes with a pouting look. Her daddy just smiled and said,

"Better get used to it, there are six more ahead of you". Lynn was not too happy with that answer, so she turned away from him and continued watching TV. Her father giggled and went back to watching TV too. Lynn's mother came to the doorway of the kitchen and yelled out to Lynn, "Did you take the last two hotdogs that were in this pan in here?" "No," Lynn said still watching TV. "Why don't you ask Stacy and her friend? There are two of them mom" she said in a smart tone. It was obvious that Lynn was fighting with her sister again, so her mother told her, "Ok, you can go upstairs and clean your side of that room, it is why you do not get a friend over this weekend." Then she went back into the kitchen.

Lynn was mad at that too, especially when her dad said, "you heard your mother, get on upstairs now." Lynn stomped off up the stairs and slammed her door. She fell on her bed, got comfortable, and started writing quietly. She thought it would drive her sister crazy if she ignored her and just acted like nothing was bothering her. Stacy and her friend stayed on her side playing music and visiting. The music was the one thing that Lynn and Stacy agreed on. This was how they passed the time until supper was ready.

"Come and eat girls!" mom yelled up the stairs. Stacy and her friend scrambled towards the door as they held Lynn back to be the last one out of the room. "Knock it off Stacy?" Lynn said as she shut the door and went downstairs. The girls gathered at the table in the kitchen, making sure that Stacy and her friend sat on the opposite side of the table. Stacy and Lynn would stretch their legs out trying to reach across and kick the other under the table. They managed to get through dinner without any major issues. Then their mom made everyone go upstairs once they were finished.

Stacy received an all-in-one disposable camera for her birthday or Christmas gift. They are one day apart so it was hard to know. However, I knew she had it, but she was not going to say anything. Night came and it was time to get ready for bed. Lynn was already afraid of under her bed because of her brothers and sisters crawling under there and grabbing her feet. They loved to pull so many pranks on her because she was the baby of the bunch. Lynn just sat in her bed listening to the music and writing until she could not hold her eyes open any longer. Stacy waited for Lynn to be in a deep sleep before they took out the hotdogs they stole earlier, and they were currently snacking on grapes too.

Stacy and her friend each took a hotdog and shoved them up Lynn's nose. This left her breathing through her mouth which leads her to snore. They took their grapes and put them in her ears, and when they were done with as much food as they could pack on Stacy took a picture! Lynn slept so hard that she did not remember a thing, so the girls had to tell Lynn what they did. "Why do I smell hotdogs"? Lynn said when she woke the next morning. "don't you remember last night"? Stacy asked. "No, what did you do Stacy"? "We put hotdogs up your nose and grapes in your ears while you were sleeping". "That explains why I smell hot dogs. And you are getting rid of that picture too." Lynn was not even awake before Stacy and Tamara were both on the floor laughing so hard at the whole situation. "You will get it Stacy and your little friend too!" Lynn said right before laying back down to sleep.

It was almost noon when the girls finally got up for the day. "Why am I smelling hotdogs?" Lynn said again, "are we having hotdogs for lunch mom?" "No," she said. "Then why am I smelling hotdogs?" Stacy and her friend were laughing like crazy now. "You don't remember Lynn?" "No, and what is so dam funny!" she said getting mad now.

"Ok, I told you this morning we put hotdogs up your nose and grapes too and then took a picture." What! Mom, did you hear that?"

"Stacy and her friend put hotdogs up my nose and took a picture with her little throw-away camera!" Stacy and her friend ran upstairs before mom could get ahold of them. "I will take care of her later." Mom said continuing to do laundry from a large mound of clothes. "I told you, you should have looked at her and her friend's mom. Two hot dogs missing, two girls at large!" Mom started to chuckle under breath so Lynn didn't think she was supportive of this behavior from the girls at all. She could not help but laugh, "Well, if you and your sister weren't too busy playing your little hotdog excursion game, we would not be having this conversation right now." That was it, Lynn had enough of her sisters' tactics.

There had to be a way to get back at her sister for being such a brat to her, but she could not think for a moment of what that would be. Until Lynn got the famous idea to ask her mom to make hotdogs for lunch that Saturday afternoon. She let Stacy think that she won and that it did not matter anymore. But, at the same time, Stacy knew better than to believe Lynn was going to just take what Stacy was dishing out. Only she did not know what to expect from Lynn.

Mom cooked the hotdogs for lunch as requested but before the other two girls could even realize what was happening, Lynn asked her mom for two hotdogs extra. "What for?" mom asked.

"Oh, just some school experiment, I can eat them after, so they don't go to waste. "Good, because we do not just throw food away around here." Lynn had what she needed to get back at these girls and they had no idea when they came down for lunch and saw that it was hotdogs for lunch Stacy and her friend had a great laugh except now the joke was going to be on Stacy. "Just remember Stacy, I said you would get yours and your little friend too." Stacy looked at Lynn with concern in her eyes because she knew that Lynn was going to get her back, but she did not know how she was going to do it. And why did mom cook hot-dogs again? Stacy was getting nervous now, but Lynn made no effort to engage with her, or giggle at her or anything, she just let her wonder.

All the girls went outside to play for the day, so they ended up for-getting about how Lynn wanted to get back at Stacy. Lynn was able to have her friends over to play just not stay the night. So that is what she did. Lynn invited a couple of friends over to play out in the yard and while they did that, they also plotted on how to get back at Stacy. When Lynn told her friends what they did to her the night before they laughed so hard. "It's not funny! I'm still smelling hotdogs!" the girls laughed even harder. "We will figure something out to get her," Jasmine said. "I already have hotdogs stashed to get them, but how? "Use them to plug her ears. They will warm up and she won't be able to hear right and take a picture as she did." She said. "Ok, that sounds good too." Lynn agreed.

Everyone went back to playing until it was dark, and the streetlights had come on. When the streetlights came on it was time to go home or check-in. If we did not do that we would hear, "Lynn, Stacy it's time to come home!" she yelled down the street. Lynn and her friends said their goodbyes and agreed to get Stacy tonight while she slept. "I will tell you how it goes in the morning. Bye." When Lynn got into the house her mother yelled from the kitchen, "Get washed up and ready for bed now." OK mom, on my way." Lynn yelled back. When Stacy saw how Lynn was being nice, doing what she was supposed to, and listening to their mother, Stacy knew something was up.

Stacy became a privet eye, watching everything Lynn did try to catch her at whatever she had planned for her. This is when Lynn went into her bed, got her writing stuff, and just sat there writing making Stacy wonder what the heck she was going to do. The girls played music like they did almost every night and hung out playing games and being goofy. It was one-thirty in the morning when Stacy and her friend finally fell asleep. Lynn got up to go to the bathroom, which was all the way downstairs but when she returned, she prepared her hotdogs in small pieces big enough to fit in Stacy's ears and nose. She quietly tiptoed over to Stacy's bed were she gently placed a hotdog piece in her ear. She rubbed over her ear like a tickle but did not knock the hotdog out. She did the rest like that too. It seemed like forever because Stacy would sleep like a pretzel and end up kicking Lynn a time or two. Lynn thought she was never going to finish, and that Stacy would catch her but nope, she got it all done, then she found Stacy's camera in her secret hiding spot. Stacy did not know that Lynn watched her the day before putting it in that spot.

Lynn went back to bed once her excursion was done and went to sleep. Everyone slept in on Sunday, except when we had to go to church. Then we took a nap after church and after we took off our good clothes. Then she heard it, "Lynn! I am going to kill you! What did you do? I cannot hear anything. It feels like wax is in my ear, but I cannot hear anything. Talk about a prank gone bad. Stacy rubbed her ear throughout the night which made the hotdog go deeper into her ear. She was getting scared when she ran to mom crying, "Mom! Lynn put hotdogs in my ears and now I cannot hear anything!" Mom sat both of her girls down at the kitchen table. "What were you thinking Lynn? This could have been worse and become a real problem." Her mom said.

"I was thinking that Stacy and her friend did nothing but pick on me and put hotdogs up my nose. I told her I was going to get her back and I did." Their mother was able to use some tweezers to put the hotdog out. "I do not want to ever see this again do you hear me?" "Yes, mother," the girls said simultaneously. "I'm sorry," Stacy said to Lynn. "I am sorry too." Do you want to go play some basketball before the boys get out there?" "Sure!" The girls made up and went to play basketball for most of the afternoon. Sisters will always be sisters and they have the best.

A Recovery Story

1 King 17:17

And it came to pass
After these things that the son of woman,
the mistress of the house fell sick
And his sickness was so sore that there was no breath left in him
King James Version Old and New Testaments

Hello, my name is Cathy and this is my recovery story. I grew up in a family of seven. I was the baby with four older sisters and two older brothers Yes, I was somewhat spoiled and usually got my way. My childhood was that of an average family. Mom was a homemaker while dad-built airplanes with a big company. Alcoholism ran in our family from my mother's side and had been passed down through generations. My grandfather had a tavern set up in his home. The back wall was nothing but alcohol shelves. In the dining room, he had the pool table and he even had the multi-colored stained-glass hanging light over the middle of the pool table. I thought it was cool. I guess you could say that was my first glamorized outlook on drinking.

Growing up, my life was normal. My elementary school years were alright, and I had a lot of friends in our neighborhood. A lot of the time, I made my sisters mad. And my brothers picked on me every chance they got. Yep, it was a normal childhood.

For as long as I can remember, I have loved paper and pens and writing poetry and lyrics. Writing just might have been the only thing I had going for me. Until I went into middle school. I always participated in school activities like band and choir, I helped in the office and volunteered every chance I had. However, comprehending my schoolwork Became harder and harder as I was becoming more and more emotional about things in my life. Mood swings set in, and I did not understand what was happening to me. I was informed that I was experiencing them just because I was a girl and that those sorts of things were going to happen. So, my mood swings were brushed under the rug.

Puberty came and went, yet those symptoms of out of control mood swings were still harping on me regularly. They started to gain their cycle and grew even more intense. I was beginning to feel like I could not understand anything, left to wonder why I was feeling this way. My behavior grew wild, I had found my voice, and I was not afraid to use it with my siblings and friends. Sometimes in school that did not work well because I would get into trouble and was often sent home. When my grades started failing, I just tried to avoid going to school at all costs, so I would not get into trouble for not being able to do the work, yet that did not work. I would still cause trouble and then get told to just go to my room and don't tell your dad.

At age eleven, I was sexually assaulted, and I spent the next year isolating and staying to myself. I tried to tell my mom about the assault, but once again, I was sent to my room and told not to tell my father. This threw the mood swings into full gear, and I began falling fast in school. I just could never grab the concept of the schoolwork; I could not understand it for the life of me. I felt discarded and alone.

I was 12 year's old when I took my first bong hit and started smoking weed. The release of the stress that I was carrying inside about myself was amazing. It masked everything I was feeling that was bad and I was not going from happy to sad in 2.2 seconds. I could handle this, or so I thought. Smoking became more and more, then on the weekends. By 13 I was drinking fifths of vodka and hanging out every chance I got. I started to smoke cigarettes too. Taking them from my dad and going to the park or wherever I could so that I would not get caught. My behavior by my 14th birthday was that of partying every chance I got. I flunked the 9th grade twice, but they sent me through anyway. My ability to comprehend and understand things never went noticed and was never dealt with. The fear of going into high school not being able to understand was a humiliation I was not going to go through.

I dropped out of school. I did nothing but hang out and party, smoke cigarettes, and think I was cool. It never came to mind to anyone that I was dealing with Bipolar and attention deficit hyperactive disorder (ADHD) and that it could have been dealt with before me falling onto the wrong path.

My mom got tired of dealing with me, so she sent me off to live with my sisters, multiple different times. My oldest sister in middle school, my second oldest sister (in Spain) when I was fourteen, (that was major party time for me too. You only had to be taller than the bar to drink no matter the age) and my third oldest sister at 16. And my fourth sister off and on in between 16 and 21. I had my first child at 21. I was still smoking weed and drinking, until one day it was suggested to put a piece of crack cocaine on top of the weed. This was all it took for me to get off and running on a 20-year dope addiction. Shortly after that first hit, I dropped the weed and went straight for the cocaine. This made me lose not only me.

First son but my two children after that to my eldest sister. My third child was my only baby girl. I was in and out of treatment centers trying to get things together, but my addiction always kept dragging me back out. When I had her, she was put into the baby ICU unit because of my crack use. I was not allowed to take her, and she went home again with my sister. I went to yet another treatment that I did not complete. Things can a bit confusing from here because I was using so often and so much. To sum it up, I married only two men, divorced only two men. The first marriage was that of a lot of drugs and a lot of physical abuse. Hiding in fear of being beaten. I had my second son at the time, and he saw me get hit with phones and anything that could hurt the most. I hid at a friend's house because we both using and it turned bad as it always did, but when he realized where I was, he busted down the door and drag me out by the hair, punching on me the whole way. The only thing I knew to do from there was to go get high again. Too embarrassed to go out or to let my family see me.

I did have moments of dry time when I would get my kids back, but it was never for long before I was back out there, and they were placed again. I was out there going from house to house getting high hanging out with only people who I knew was getting high. I eventually went from crack cocaine to meth. Drinking and smoking weed was few and far between or when I was coming down and I did not want to hurt too badly. Meth took over from there and that is when I lost everything that ever meant anything, husband (of ten years) kids, home, and most of all me.

It became a mission every day and night to go and find the next high. If the dope was not available, I was drinking. Sometimes it was anywhere from 2 to 8, 40oz of beer at a time, including early morn-ings. I was borrowing from anyone I could. I was stealing from family to feed my addiction, selling off everything I could just to get a sack. I was considered a bag hoe because I was even willing to give myself in dangerous positions just to get the next high. I was having my mother come watch my kids (when I did have them) at 2 or 3 in the morning with some lame excuse just so I could make a drug run. I had no respect for anything not even myself. I cared about nothing, not even me. I lied at every turn because I did not want anyone to know what I was doing. I did not want to be another disappointment to my mother.

I eventually ended up sleeping in my car, my husband made sleep in my car in the apartment building behind his house because I was not allowed there anymore. When that broke down, I was on the bus living out of a motel room. Many reports were made on me, 8 years after my daughter I had another boy that ended up with his father from the triage department at the local hospital. That was another excuse for me to go get high again. So, off and running yet again. I finally ended up pregnant for the last time with the boy I have now. Even though when I had him my last husband was there for us (it was not his child) momentarily until I went from the motel room to my apartment. The biological father stepped up and claimed his son. I was still using and getting into trouble until it came down to the decision of, either run off to another state with his biological father and end up with a war-rant and my child taken or face the music and take my son and me to a six-month treatment center to get the help I truly needed. I did not know anyone in the other state and feared to make such a move, so I gave up my house, packed up what we needed, and went to treatment.

Once settled into the Evergreen Manor Women's and Children Inpatient Treatment Center in Everett Washington www.evergreenmanor.

org it felt like jail to me because we were getting searched and what we were not able to have was taken. I was in a place that I did not know because I was ready to be done with this slow suicide, I had been placing on myself for so many years.

This was the do or die moment for me. I was numb, I just stared at my son with nothing. Tears started to roll down my check but there was no sound. I put my boy in the crib once the lady left, he began to fuss and wanted me, but I just could not. I could not move even though I felt the teardrops fall onto my hand. I pushed all our belongings aside, slowly stood taking off my shoes. I walked around to the end of the bed and dropped to my knees. Many times, I asked God selfishly to get me out of situations and I would never do it again. That was a lie. This time was different. The tears were crocodile tears by now, then I took a deep breath, paused, and what came out of me next even shocked me. "Lord, I am ready, sick, and tired of being sick and tired. I am at your mercy. Please remove the taste of dope from my mouth, the craving for drugs and alcohol from my body, and remove the people I used with from my path. Please heal this body so that I can be a better person for me, my son, and those who love me. I am ready to surrender my every fiber to you and my recovery. Thank you, Lord, for seeing that I did not die out there. I know you have a plan for me even though I do not know what that is, I am ready to follow that path. Amen!"

It was not easy for the first couple of months after that. I wanted to leave and run but I asked the counselors to please sit on me at all cost because this is what I do, and I wanted my recovery this time. They did just that. I was welcome to leave any time I wanted to, but my child was going to have to stay there. I was not having that. They put child protective services (CPS) on my case and I made it through the rough part. It was so hard! Both of us got sick and it was miserable. Two and a half weeks stuck in a room with a sick baby while I was not only sick from the drug withdrawal but the bug my son and I caught but, I made it through that. I then called home to learn that my husband had finally left me for other women and had moved her into what I thought was to be my home when I got out. This was my first love at 19 and all I knew. This hurt my soul, but I had to work through it. About a month or so later I received a phone call from my son's biological grandmother in another state telling me that my son's father had died due to an overdose.

Emotionally I could not handle this, with what I had learned prior and now this! I dropped the phone and fell from the chair I was sitting in, screaming, and crying so hard they had to take my son to another room, so it did not scare him. These two events were more than I could take. I lost it! Screaming very loudly "Oh my God no! Please God say it isn't so!" "I cannot do this flipping crap! My husband left me and now my baby's daddy! I don't want to do this anymore!" "Please God just take me too!" "Protect my children and please take me they don't need someone like me, please give them better than I have!" Grasping for air was all I could at this moment. I have never in my life felt such a pain as I did that day and did not use it over it.

It must have been weeks that passed before the tears stopped. Every day all day, crying, sitting through classes crying. The nights were horrible! Nightmares of being left and/or dying out there in the drug world. What did he go through? Who was he with? Did they try to save him at all? I even beat myself up for the longest time because I chose to go to treatment and not go with him. Had I gone with him, could I have saved him? Would be dead too? If he were using, I would have been too. Was it the bad drugs that killed him? Was it the fact he had a bad heart already? What would have become of my son? The ultimate question was... was it my fault he was using and died?

I will never know. I do not think it was even a week or two, time was so blurry through all this. I could not even keep up with the day of the week. One of the ladies who had an infant there, slept with her three-week-old baby on a boppy pillow next to her in the bed, which we were not allowed to do. To only wake up the next morning to find her baby dead under the pillow beside her. She was only 19 and the whole center was in mourning for some time. We had a spiritual ceremony in the room where she passed, smudged the whole building, and was provided counseling on a crisis level because of all that had been going on. I sat on the edge of my bed at 2:30 am hearing the cries of a young mother who believed she killed her newborn baby.

What I had just gone through did not seem as bad as what this lady was going through. I got the opportunity to hold her, trying to convince her that it was not her fault this happened. She looked me dead in my eyes and screamed "I killed my baby! I killed my baby!" The pain I felt earlier was nothing compared to the pain I saw that night. For the next couple of days, it was somber and incredibly sad for everyone. That lady eventually left the center and we did not hear anything else about her. I was left to regain strength at every place I could find it.

This is when I started talking to God regularly. Every night I would talk with him asking so many questions as to why all these things were happening and what was it that we were to learn from this. I concluded that we are not promised tomorrow. I saw my son through different eyes after that. A little fearful of the night because anything can happen in a short amount of time. I found myself holding him a little tighter the next day, and even though I was as heavy as I have been in my heart and soul, I heard, If you can make it through all this without running back to drugs and alcohol, you are strong enough to make it through anything. With every bad moment I may have, I tell myself that it is not as bad as what I went through during that period of my life. So much in such a short period. I thanked God for that night over and over and over.

I just knew in my heart that something might have been wrong with the baby or a situation he has foreseen that made it necessary for God to take his angel so early.

I found myself in a very unfamiliar place now. I was experiencing gratitude sober and at the same time something was happening not only in me but around me that I often did not understand, things so unexplainable that you could only look up and say thank you. I went from, I cannot do this it is not me too, and with you God I know I can. It was so amazing how different it was this time when I spoke to God. I felt my connection return to him even though I was baptized and saved about four or five years earlier. They did not think I was going to snap out of the mental state that meth or loss, or death can put a person in, I was in that "fog" for a few months, but they stayed right by me the whole way until I did. This too shall pass, I kept hearing. I was never ready to stop using all the other times I went into recovery, but all of this was different. The way that they taught me how to read my body when I was getting ready to relapse and the patterns that I had leading up to that relapse.

It made a huge difference the way the treatment center taught you to look at your disease as a medical condition and how to deal with the underlining issues, such as bipolar so that I did not have to mask the problems by self-medicating with street drugs and alcohol. A chemical imbalance of the brain can be balanced by proper medication under a doctor's care so that I did not have to use street drugs to feel normal. It made all the difference in the world to me to have my vision changed like that.

I believe that being able to look at myself like that made it easier to accept who and what I am so that I could begin working my way back to the real me. Classes, five days a week, from 8 am to 5 pm for six months was the plan in the beginning. Because I was sincere from the heart with God, I felt him with me the whole way this time. I went from, "why me"? To "what are you trying to teach me here"? That attitude allowed me to push ahead and shine more than ever. I am a little bit of a control freak about me and mine, so I rose into leadership positions for our section and was able to graduate a month early for an amazing bounce back.

Later on, in treatment I did ask God for a house with a fenced-in yard and rose bushes outside, superficial I know, but when I left Evergreen Manor I chose to go into an Oxford house for women and children so that I could remain clean. It was my hometown and stomping grounds were only an effort away. I needed that extra structure. I arrived at the house to see an amazing big red house. It had a privacy fence all around the huge back yard. Rose bushes lined the front of the house and a couple was scattered in the back yard as well. No one knew of this but me and God so when I saw this, I instantly had tears in my eyes. The worker who drove me there from Everett had no idea what I had just experienced.

After settling in at the Oxford house, it was only about a month before I was ready to leave there too but I prayed every day for God to see me through this and stay with me because now was going to be the time I either made it strong or ran back to active addiction. It was too easy now. I thought there no case for my son because there was no contact with social services except the one time, they spoke to me in treatment when I wanted to leave. I stayed for two years in that house loving almost every moment. At that time.

I was working with wonderful people from the state who helped me get back into the world. Then one day out of the blue a worker came to the house unexpectedly to touch base with me about my son. There was no contact from these people whatsoever the whole time I was in treatment or out until this day. He came in and said he needed to do a status update for us.

He walked through my place, looked in the cupboards, checked out my son, and did a series of questions that would impress an interrogation officer. After I showed him every certificate of completion that I had from treatment, outpatient, counseling, parenting, and status of the house. I was treasurer of the whole house currently. He said there was no need to go any further and that he would just close the case. Had I not been doing well; things would not have gone so well. Ironically, every person I was working with had a similar story to mine and a connection to God like no other.

I started achieving things like getting my license back which I never really had in the first place. Completing my GED so that I could go on to college and making sure that my son was in a good daycare and make sure that he was ready for the right school. I finally moved out into my place continuing with my education. A couple of relationships have come and gone but I have gone as far as I could with my education, I made it to 72% of my bachelor's degree in business management and I look forward to finishing it soon.

As of today, I have ten years in recovery, we have our little two-bedroom apartment where I care for my son and raise my granddaughter. I have started with my writing again in hopes to get that to go somewhere. I would love the music industry, but we all know how hard that would be. I just love to do it, so for now, I will use it for my passion and hobby. I hope by sharing this story that it might save another addict's life. Letting others know they are not alone, and they do not have to face the challenges alone. Active addiction can feel like there is no hope and I am living proof that there is.

God felt I was worth every moment he gave me to fight. I grew strong and today I fight for every moment God gives me because now I believe I am worth every one of them moments too. Thank you for taking the time to read my story and may God bless us all.

CRITTER ON THE ROOF

Genesis 9:2

And the fear of you and you dread of you
Shall be upon every beast of the earth
And upon every fowl of the air upon all that moveth upon the earth
And upon all the fishes of the sea into your hand, they are delivered
King James Version Old and New Testaments

I t was a hot summer day and the pool was just about full. Brendon had mentioned to his father Mason more than once about that critter on the roof that seems to like the fireplace chimney. It was not a major problem right then, so Mason blew it off. "OK dad, you should listen about the critters, the other night I came face to face with a raccoon!" "They are not going to bother you if you don't bother them just leave them alone." His father replied. "Ok," Brendon said, and then he went to do his own thing.

It seemed odd around that house because the wild animals loved it. Squirrels, racoons, cats, even a dog got under the house. One time they were looking out to the back yard and saw a whole flock of about one-hundred or more small birds burying themselves in the sand around the pool. The cats like to lay up against the pool to keep cool, and the dog down the alleyway just loves to charge at you barking his head off like he is about to do some damage but if you yell at him, he will turn around and run back home and over the fence. Thank goodness that no one has ever been hurt by that dog, yet. With all the critters around there, it's nothing new to hear something running across the roof of the house now and then, but not for one minute did anyone in that house expect this.

Mason and Brendon were gone most of the day with work and school. But when it was time to get home, Mason came through the back door like he did every day and was standing at the table just outside the kitchen. He went to sit down on the couch and suddenly stops dead in his tracks! That little squirrel managed to fall down the chimney and was sitting up on the mantle of the fireplace. It was looking at Mason not moving a muscle, the squirrel looked like a statue up there until he stood up and put whatever he had to his mouth. Mason was out! He instantly turned around and headed for the door. He already had a fear of rodents and this surely qualified. He quickly went out back and came around to the front of the house to open the doors and windows so that he could try to get it out from the outside. That squirrel was not moving, and he looked to be enjoying his time inside.

Meanwhile, Mason stayed outside until Brendon got home. Brendon was still in his teens, but he loved to grab the broom for any critter problems that may arise. "What are you doing outside dad"? Brendon asked. "There's a dam squirrel in the house"! Mason said. "What the hell"? Brendon said. "Yep, a squirrel fell down the chimney now we have to figure out how to get it out"! They went to see what the squirrel was up to and it was gone from the mantle. Mason and Brendon crept around the house trying to peek in to see if they could see him. With broom in hand now, Brendon was ready for what came his way. They opened the back doors for an easy escape as they started in the house. The kitchen was clear, and the living room was more like a game of "Can you find it?"

Mason went further into the living room slowly. Then he started down the hallway towards the bathroom when he heard something coming from the bathroom. Brendon stepped up with the broom. He slowly got to the bathroom door and with it held high he began to peek around the door. "AAAAA" Brendon screamed in high pitch scream, then suddenly slammed the door. "It is in the bathroom dad! It's trying to climb the shower curtain!" "Ok, keep that door shut boy and we can open the window from outside I think, maybe he will go out the window". Mason told him.

The squirrel was in the bathtub scratching around trying to find a way his way out. Brendon was going to the door again and ended upcoming face to face with the little critter, it scared the squirrel even more. Brendon was still carrying the broom in combat mode, ready for anything as this critter kept jumping crazy around the bathroom. Mason was not thrilled at all with the way the critter got in the house in the first place. Every night you could hear it scurry across the roof and hang around the chimney. Now and again little crumbs would fall down the chimney making a mess.

Brendon decided to try to open the bathroom door again. Suddenly the squirrel jumped at the door making this horrible screech sound, "AAAA" Brendon screamed this time in a high, loud tone sounding like a goat yelling. Mason was laughing at Brendon at this point trying to get ahold of this critter. He put the broom into the bathroom trying to hit the squirrel to push him out the window, but it did not work because the squirrel was jumping all over trying to find a way out. Brendon kept trying to open the door and using the broom but that only made it crazier until he finally was able to jump onto the curtains to the window that was open and found a way out.

Brendon was still afraid to go in the bathroom even though the squirrel managed to find a way out. He was still freaking out at the door, squealing like a goat. Mason kept his distance at the front of the house and when the squirrel jumped on the curtain he ran back into the house and shut the door quickly. The squirrel finally jumped out the window and ran up into the tree.

That evening Brendon and Mason were sitting watching TV when they both heard the little pitter-pat of another critter on the roof. They both looked at each other and shook their heads. While Mason moved towards the fireplace, Brendon grabbed the broom he had sitting next to him just in case. The critter was still on the roof, but Mason was not going to have him fall into the house again. He quickly shut the air vent and placed an exceptionally large piece of cardboard across the whole front of the fireplace itself.

Brendon just sat there with his broom and when his father turned around to see him sitting in combat mode, he just laughed at him and said, "That's a lazy man." Brendon giggled and said, we are supposed to work smarter not harder dad." They both laughed but that did not mean Brendon was going to put the broom down either. "OK, I think he went to the back of the house now," Mason said as returned to his comfortable position on the couch.

"I am not taking any chances dad," Brendon said as he got up. "I am checking out back too." He added. "I don't think you should be poking your nose around out there; you don't know if it's gone or not," Mason told him. "I know," Brendon told his dad but that did not stop him from going out to the back door and opening it to see what was out there. It was later in the evening, so it was kind of dark and he did not have a flashlight or anything to help him see. Brendon goes stepping out the back door and all Mason heard was a screech out of Brendon, "AAAAAA! Dad, I do not know what to do, I am face to face with a raccoon and I am not moving! Daaad!" "Just slowly walk back into the house as if it's nothing and he won't hurt you. If nothing else shoo him away like a cat or something".

Brendon turned around and leaped back into the house freaked out by what just happened. He was only supposed to be seeing that little squirrel and met something bigger. He took his broom and stayed his behind in the house after that. He came in and sat in the living room with his dad, "you should have seen how big that thing was"! He said to his dad, "and you didn't even answer me when I called for you!" Mason chuckled and said, "Told you not to go poking your nose out there, now he got his friends on you." They both laughed at his little joke, but Brendon was not taking any more chances. He locked all doors and windows and made sure that Mason covered the fireplace well enough.

He checked all the rooms, especially the bathroom, and closed all doors. Brendon spent the night hanging out with Mason until he fell asleep. Mason could not help but smile when he looked over to Brendon sleeping so peacefully, with his broom next to him. He was ready for any one of those critters on the roof.

A FEELING FOR FOREVER

Deuteronomy 33:12

And of the Benjamin he said,
The beloved of the Lord shall dwell in safety by him;
And the Lord shall cover him all day long
And he shall dwell between his shoulders

*I*t was such a young love. No one believed they loved each other enough for it to be true love. But they showed them. Braxton and Brandy were nineteen and twenty years old. The very moment they laid eyes on each other they knew this one was going to be the one or was it? Braxton met Brandy at a social gathering a few months back and they only got closer and closer the more they saw each other. In the evening time, Braxton would call Brandy and talk with her for hours at a time until someone yelled, they needed to use it. Brandy did not have to worry about Braxton and other girls, for the most part. He was incredibly good with her and kept it real. Yep, even after the honeymoon stage. The first two years were magical! There was not anything that could come between these two. He was working hard in construction and Brandy was working for a rancher tending to show horses. This meant that long days were coming, and it was not going to be easy on either one of them.

One day they got home around the same time, he kissed her hello like he did every day. "We deserve a short vacation babe; don't you think so?" Brandy started this conversation and Braxton quickly turned his head to look at Brandy like she was crazy. I thought we could go down to the beach for a night or two, just the two of us. Please." Brandy said in a sweet tone trying to convince him to go. "I'll think about it," Braxton said as he finished taking off his work boots. "OK fine." It was only the beginning of the week, so Braxton took his sweet old time on giving Brandy her answer. This was extremely frustrating for Brandy because she is a planner.

As the week took off Brandy was feeling OK. She made it to work a couple of days when she began to feel ill. She made it through and then had to call in for a day. On Wednesday, Braxton came home in a great mood. Kissing and hugging Brandy while picking her up. "Put me down babe my stomach hurts." "Oh, OK honey sorry, you OK?" he asked her. "Yes, I'm fine just a little yucky." She replied. He looked at her with concern but did not want to fuss. "If you want to go to the beach this weekend, I took it off for us to go." He said smiling at her. He was trying to make her smile too, but all she could think about was hitting the bathroom, feeling like she was going to throw up. "Here honey I will fix you some homemade chicken soup and crackers." Braxton said.

He kissed her on the forehead then got up and went into the kitchen to begin preparing to cook. It was about ten minutes later when nothing was stopping her now, straight to the bathroom. When she came back, she just chalked it up to having a stomach bug. "Well, this right here will cure you, sweetheart," Braxton said teasing her into a smile. "Here is your favorite blanket, get better food and we can enjoy new movies tonight." "Thank you, honey, you're the best" as she kissed him. They got comfortable on the couch so they could cuddle up and eat their homemade chicken soup together.

The next couple of days went as normal. Brandy was not so sick anymore, but she was curious about her stomach bug so on Thursday evening she decided to take a pregnancy test, just to rule it out. OK, that was the longest two minutes of Brandy's life. She sat on the bathtub hesitating to look, so many things going through her head. She slowly looked down into her lap and held the stick up to read it. Brandy almost fell over into the tub when that stick told her she was pregnant, and Braxton was going to be a father for the first time. She was excited and scared at the same time. Then she hid the box and started getting things together for their weekend away.

The next morning, they were supposed to be leaving for the beach. *That will be the best place to tell him the good news.* She thought to herself.

Without a word said between them, there were more smiles than there has been ever. "What are you so smiley for? Braxton asked. "Nothing babe, I'm just really happy. My stomach bug is better, and we get to go to the beach just the two of us. I am looking forward to some much-needed quality time. Maybe we can rent horses on the beach for an hour. Just saying." "Rent horses"? Braxton asked. "Yeah, where we use to go when I was little has a spot where you can rent to ride a horse for an hour or two. It was a lot of fun. I loved riding on the beach it was the best." Brandy told him. "OK," Braxton said, looking at her crazy because she was the total opposite from yesterday and she has a lot more get up and goes. Little did he know of the surprise Brandy had for him.

That night when they went to bed Brandy rolled over so they could have their nightly pillow talk. "Thank you." She said and then softly kissed his cheek. "What was that for?" Braxton asked. "It was for everything you do for us here and out there working," she replied. "I love you more than anything in this world, you know that?" she said snuggling up next to him. "I love you too honey." He said in a whisper. It was so hard for her not to say anything to him about the baby. He kissed her goodnight and they drifted off to sleep in each other's arms.

It was the best morning ever after Brandy threw up her breakfast. She was trying to hide it from Braxton and so far, she was doing a fairly good job at it. They both got up, "good morning honey" Braxton said. "Good morning baby, it is beautiful for our trip today, so we better get on it, so we don't waste the day away." Brandy told him. "OK," Braxton said. They packed up the truck, made sure they had all their traveling music, double checked everything, and started on a two-hour drive.

Braxton was planning to surprise Brandy with a beach house vacation. Brandy is thinking they are going to be camping out and Braxton had already planned through his work for them to use a beach house for the weekend. Braxton loved Brandy more than anything in his world and he would do almost anything for her. Brandy was the same way about Braxton.

Brandy turned the music on low at first, but the radio station was playing good music, so she started singing along. Another song would come on, and Braxton could not help but start singing too. Next thing you know they are singing together, missing words, singing off-key, and laughing the whole way.

The closer they drove towards the water Brandy could smell the water. She was one who was able to give a sense of smell to water.

"You're weird, do you know that?" Braxton said to her smiling. "Yes, I am aware of my talents!" She said confidently and playful. They began to laugh with each other. They were coming up to a little town, "Look, Braxton, it is so beautiful." she said looking at all the sidewalk shops on both sides of the street. It was quaint with history but had some modern style to it too. "OK," Braxton said. It was not a big thing for him, but she loved to see places she had never seen before. "We are almost there, pick your tongue up and stop drooling honey". Braxton said giggling a little under his breath. The next town was just off the ocean itself. It was great for Brandy and Braxton knew right then she was going to be happy with what he had planned for them. She was wondering, "Where in the heck are you going?" she asked very curiously? Then instantly turned her attention to the wonderful view of the ocean and the waves crashing up onto land. "Wow Braxton, this place is magical." And about that time, he turned up into the driveway of a large beach house and parked. They were shocked when they saw that it was a cabin-like house just off the beach. "What are we doing here Braxton? This is not where we were supposed to be going." She said. Starting to panic that her plans were going to be ruined. "We are supposed to be here honey. Surprise! It has been approved through work honey for us to spend two nights here with an oceanfront view".

"Really babe?" "Yeah honey that's why I said we could even go," Braxton told her. "Wow! honey, this place is amazing." It was everything she could think of and more. Brandy was thinking that her plan was going to be even better. There was a restaurant just down the street, so they did not have to go far for dinner.

They arrived at the restaurant and offered her the window seat. He wanted her to enjoy everything that the evening had to offer. This is all so amazing honey". Brandy said. The view was amazing, and the man was amazing too. While enjoying their meal under soft lights, music playing in the background, and the Pacific Ocean just outside the window, Braxton stood up and walked over to Brandy. He got down one knee and she instantly started crying she was so happy. "I love you more than anything in this world and I would love to spend the rest of my life with you, Brandy, will you marry me?" Braxton asked. "Yes, of course, I will honey, I love you so much." She replied. Braxton was so happy he picked her up and twirled her around. "Honey?" Brandy said. "Yes," Braxton said. "I'm going to throw up." Braxton immediately put her down and backed away. They sat back down holding hands across the table, more in love than ever before, then they enjoyed a wonderful meal together.

The sun was getting ready to set. It was deep red and mesmerizing. They shared a piece of the pie when Braxton asked, "Would you like to go for a walk on the beach before turning in for the evening?" Brandy could not stop smiling and the night was only about to get better. This was going to work out for Brandy better than she thought it would. "Yes, I would"." That would be wonderful." Brandy said. She started to get nervous now because she was about to tell him they were pregnant, and she did not know what his reaction was going to be.

On the walk down to the beach Brandy kept thinking to herself, *I hope this does not ruin the night, please be happy about this*. This was going to be a lot to take in for one night. They reached the sand then took their shoes off. The sand was refreshingly cool. Braxton held her hand as they made it down by the water. Walking along hand in hand, Braxton? Brandy asked. "Yes," he replied. "I have never been happier than I am right now at this moment." She said. Braxton held her closer to him and said, "I am glad to hear that cause, so am I?" 'The proposal was beautiful and right on time sweetheart, this night couldn't have gone any more perfect." They were facing each other now holding each other arm in arm as the sun was slowly going down. Just before the last of the sun was to go over the horizon Brandy looked at Braxton and said, "Not only am I a going to be your wife honey, you are going to be a father."

Braxton let go of Brandy and was now holding her by her upper arms looking into her eyes like laser beams. Brandy started to giggle because she thought he was going to freak out. "I am going to be a dad. Brandy?" "Yes baby, we are going to have a baby. I found out yesterday and have been dying to tell you." Braxton held Brandy to his chest, I love you. This couldn't have gotten any better for both of us sweetheart," he said. "You have made me the happiest man in the entire world today. I don't need anything but you, me, and our baby." Braxton said holding her close to him. He kissed her softly then took her hand as they walked on together side by side without a word said. Until Braxton suddenly let go of Brandy's hand and began running and yelling, "I'm going to be a dad"! Brandy started laughing, loving the fact they were both so happy about everything. The sunset and chemistry between them right now could not have been more special.

They reached the back entryway to their place. "Honey look at this place." Brandy said slowly walking up into the back area where there was a brick fireplace with a firepit. It was surrounded by marble countertops on both sides. It was amazing. It was not their wedding night, but it might as well have been because Braxton picked Brandy up and carried her into the house. Once inside Brandy looked at Braxton and he said, "It was just too perfect not to honey".

There was a modern theme inside the house even though it was a cabin, there were things like an electric fireplace and espresso machine. It was amazing too. Just enough to have the country of the cabin and just enough amenities of today to make it perfect. Braxton and brandy just sat down in the living room and held each other for a while. They were enjoying the fact that you can open the curtains on the west side of the house and watch the ocean out the window up close and personal from where they sat. Brandy kept looking at her ring and Braxton kept his hand on her stomach. There was a smile on his face that was ear to ear. "What are you smiling for?" Brandy asked him. "This right here, this is a feeling for forever honey, and I am enjoying my forever right here," Braxton told her. "I love you, sweetheart. Thank you for the most wonderful day a girl could ever ask for." Brandy replied. "I love you both too," Braxton said.

This was a day that gave a feeling that could last forever. It was not every day that you became a mother and a wife and for him, a husband, and a father all on the same evening. Brandy kept thinking back on her wonderful day as she watched Braxton off and on. It kept going over and over in Brandy's mind that her family was just now built in a day and over dinner no less. Neither one of them knew of the other plans but the way that the whole day has been one magical moment after another has been mesmerizing.

They sat in silence while the waves crashed against the shore and the smell of sea air was just enough of a getaway to feel relaxed finally. "This was the most perfect day." Brandy whispered as she laid up against his chest looking out the window. "And you're my perfect one" Braxton whispered back. They cuddled in tighter to enjoy the ocean waves and each other. It had been such an emotional day for both, they took that forever feeling and fell asleep to it on the couch.

It was magical. The whole day was magical! This was the moment that felt so surreal. It was their feeling for forever. "Thank you, God."

Brandy whispered to herself before drifting off to sleep, after the most perfect day, in Braxton's arms

The End

Special Thanks to

GOD
For saving my life and
helping me when I could not help myself

My family
Mr. and Mrs. Ralph and Nancy Woolhouse,
Terrie, Nancy Debbie, Jim, Pat, and Shelly,
Thank you for always being there,
I will never forget you.
Thank you for teaching me how to take a chance on me
And all the unconditional love
Throughout my life

Evergreen Manor and Oxford housing,
www.evergreenmanor.com
www.oxfordhouse.com
Thank you for giving me the structure required
To have a better life.

And

Mr. Andre Cole
Management/consultant
Intelligent Productions

Thank you for believing in me,
And always being there to help with
management, mentoring, consulting, and guidance
with my first book Her Way Home

The stories from this wonderful author are uplifting, inspiring, and funny.

Life can have some funny moments as well. It is easy to share the struggle but we mustn't forget the good times that got us here. These are only some of the stories to come that can show you that there is life after trauma, and those moments are the ones that make all the madness worth it. These clips in time are based on true stories that helped me get to where I am today with a smile on my face. These stories will touch your heart and leave you crying with laughter. God and the laughter are what got me through It has been a pleasure writing for you and I look forward to writing more in the future.

For more great reading and media contact
Go to www.cathisvisions.org or
wwww.intelligentproductions.com

CPSIA information can be obtained
at www.ICGtesting.com
Printed in the USA
JSHW031347240621
16207JS00005B/141